On My Own

3

MW01598867

On My Own

3

**Comprehension Response Activities
to Accompany**
- *Spreading My Wings*
- *Tales—Princesses, Peas, and Enchanted Trees*
- *Beneath the Surface*
- *Super Senses!*
- *Carving New Frontiers*

AUTHORS

Ron Benson
Iris Zammit

REVIEWERS

Veda Hanninen, Copper Cliff, Ontario
Jodi Mackie, Edmonton, Alberta
Lynn Swanson, Surrey, British Columbia

Toronto

Publisher: Kathleen Doyle
Content Editor: Jenny Armstrong
Coordinating Editor: Anne MacInnes
Production Coordinator: Stephanie Cox
Permissions: Michaele Sinko
Cover and Interior Design: ArtPlus Ltd.
Page Layout: Barb Neri/ArtPlus Ltd.

COLLECTIONS 3 **Author Team**
Ron Benson
Lynn Bryan
Kim Newlove
Charolette Player
Liz Stenson

ACKNOWLEDGEMENTS
Every reasonable effort has been made to find copyright holders for material contained in this book. In the case of any omissions, the Publisher would be pleased to make suitable acknowledgements in future editions.

Illustrations
Page 13: Jock MacRae; 15, 59: Bill Kimber; 23, 39, 75: Vesna Krstanovich; 25, 33, 37: Paul Wiersma; 61: Sami Suomolain; 77: June Bradford

Photos
Page 49: Corel Stock Photo Library

Copyright © 2001 Pearson Education Canada Inc., Toronto, Ontario
All rights reserved. This publication is protected by copyright, and permission should be obtained from the publisher prior to any prohibited reproduction, storage in a retrieval system, or transmission in any form or by any means, electronic, mechanical, photocopying, recording, or likewise. For information regarding permission, write to the Permissions Department.

ISBN 0-13-090315-9

1 2 3 4 5 W 05 04 03 02 01

Contents

To accompany *Tales—Princesses, Peas, and Enchanted Trees*

To accompany *Beneath the Surface*

To accompany *Super Senses!*

To accompany *Building Community*

Reader Response — For these activities, you reread one of the selections in your *COLLECTIONS* book and answer questions about it.

Reading Mini Lesson — These activities are two pages long. On one of the pages there is a new selection to read. The questions on the other page give you a chance to practise a skill your teacher taught in a lesson.

Memo

To: *COLLECTIONS* readers
From: The authors
Subject: What you need to know about the **On My Own** book

On My Own has activities to go along with selections in your *COLLECTIONS* book, as well as for some new selections. The activities will give you an opportunity to use the skills you are learning as a reader, writer, and thinker.

We have put the answers at the back of your book in a pull-out section. When you finish each activity, you can check your answers and record the results on a "How Did I Do?" chart. This chart will give you an idea of how well you are doing with the activities.

Read "How to Use This Book" on the next page, and "How to Self-Check Your Work" on page 96, to learn more about using **On My Own**.

Good luck! Write to us on the *COLLECTIONS* website (www.pearsoned.ca/collections) to let us know how well you are doing.

How to Use the *On My Own* Book

Here you find out **what to read**. You will be asked to read a selection in your *COLLECTIONS* book, or you will read a new selection in the *On My Own* book, before you do the page.

Here is a **tip** to help you think about the activity.

Reading for Meaning

Authors use words to give you a certain "picture." You may need to think carefully about the meaning of some words to really understand what the author is saying.

This part tells you **what to do**.

1. Reread "Our Home Is the Sea" to find the sentences below.
2. Change the underlined word to the one that is closest in meaning.
3. Rewrite the sentence.

Example: I am the eldest son. (only, oldest, odd)
     I am the oldest son.

This shows you **how to do it**.

1. I stuff my report card into a pocket. (crash, cram, fold)

_____

2. A mother with a baby strapped on her back bends down. (tied, tucked, lying)

Write your answers here.

_____

3. I hurry down the stairs and get off. (hop, jump, rush)

_____

4. As quietly as I can, I walk past the old man. (quickly, noiselessly, bravely)

Go to page 96 to find out how to do the self-checking.

_____

5. The night mist falls gently down as we eat. (softly, suddenly, heavily)

How Did I Do?
Check your answers with those on page 97 and fill in the chart on page 100.

> **More to Do**
> Write 2 or more words that mean the same as
> **1. quickly**
> **2. spread**
> Check the dictionary meaning of your 2 words.
>
> ### My Self-Check
> I wrote 2 words for **quickly.** . . . . ☐
> I wrote 2 words for **spread.** . . . . ☐
> I checked the dictionary meanings. ☐

There is an extra activity on some pages for you to do. Do it on a sheet of paper or in your notebook. You can share this work with a partner or your teacher.

To accompany "Our Home Is the Sea"

SPREADING MY WINGS 17

Check here to be sure you have done every part of the activity.

Identifying Ideas

Authors of poems do not always put capital letters and periods to help you to read new ideas in sentences. You may need to reread the poem to decide where each idea begins and ends.

1. Read "September Jitters."

2. Identify the ideas in Stanzas 2 and 3 and list them.

Stanza 1

Examples:	
Idea 1	I'm wearing my brand new sneakers.
Idea 2	A new barrette's in my hair.
Idea 3	This shirt is a gift from Grandma.
Idea 4	I'm almost ready to go.

Stanza 2

Idea 5	
Idea 6	
Idea 7	
Idea 8	

Stanza 3

Idea 9	
Idea 10	
Idea 11	
Idea 12	
Idea 13	

3. Which idea tells you that the girl has the "jitters"?

_____

How Did I Do?

Check your answers with those on page 97 and fill in the chart on page 100.

September Jitters

I'm wearing my brand new sneakers
A new barrette's
In my hair
This shirt is a gift from Grandma
I'm almost ready . . .
To go.

Mom gives me a treat for recess
And I pick up
My baseball mitt
Dad counts me out my lunch money
I'm almost ready . . .
To go.

I run down the street to the corner
I see the bus
Stop at the light
I hope I have everything with me
I'm almost ready . . .
I'm gone!

To accompany "September Yearning"

Learning About Characters

Thinking about how characters feel helps you to understand the characters you read about. You can find the proof of their feelings by reading what they do and say.

1. Read "Not the Only One."
2. Read the sentences in the first column.
3. Write the sentence that proves each feeling. Write the proof in the second column. Use the list of Proofs below the columns.

Feeling	Proof
Example: Ben felt nervous.	He wasn't excited. He was going to a new school.
1. Ben felt worried.	
2. Ben felt disappointed.	
3. Ben felt happy.	
4. Ben felt shy.	
5. Ben felt confident.	

Proofs

He wasn't excited. He was going to a new school.	His stomach was doing flip-flops and he bit his lip.
	He smiled and waved back.
He held his head high as he went into school.	He didn't say "Hi."
	His shoulders drooped.

How Did I Do?

Check your answers with those on page 97 and fill in the chart on page 100.

More to Do

Think about a time you had one of the feelings in the first column. Write about that time. Tell about where you were, who was there, and what happened.

My Self-Check

I thought about a feeling I had. . . . .❑

I wrote about
- where I was . . . .❑
- who was there . . . .❑
- what happened . . . .❑

To accompany "Home Early"

Not the Only One

Every other year, Ben could hardly wait for school to begin. Today he wasn't excited. He was going to a new school. His family had just moved and he didn't know anyone yet. He didn't even know how to find his way around the school to Room 24 and Mrs. Mac!

"Are you sure you don't want me to come with you, Ben?" asked Mom.

"Definitely not, Mom! I'm almost nine. I'll be fine," he said. But he didn't feel fine. His stomach was doing flip-flops and he was biting his lip.

All too soon it was time to leave, and when Mom gave him his goodbye hug, he didn't want her to let go. But he straightened his shoulders and set off down the street. He saw the letter carrier drop letters into the house across the street. He crossed over and asked her if any kids lived there. The letter carrier told him, "No." Ben's shoulders drooped.

As he turned the corner, he saw the bus pull up at the stop. Lots of kids got off. Ben hurried to catch up with them, wondering if any of them would be in his class. One boy looked back and waved to Ben. Ben smiled and waved back. He wanted to say "Hi" but he didn't.

Ben followed the kids down the road and, before he knew it, he was at the school. There were lots of kids in the yard, and teachers too. Everyone was talking and laughing. Ben felt the butterflies fluttering in his stomach. "No one else looks nervous," thought Ben. "I must be the only new kid."

Just then the boy who had waved to him came over. "Hi," he said. "Are you new at this school? Whose class are you in?" When Ben told him he was in Mrs. Mac's, the boy answered, "Neat. I'm in her class too. We can go in together. I'm always a bit nervous about going to a new class and a new teacher. I'm Jordy. What's your name?"

Ben smiled as he told him.

The bell rang. It was time to go into class. Ben held his head high as he followed Jordy to Room 24. The teacher smiled as each kid came through the door and put on a name tag. When it was Ben's turn, she said, "Hi, Ben! You're new here, aren't you? Guess what—so am I, and I'm a bit nervous! Who's your friend?"

Ben smiled at his new friend and said, "Mrs. Mac, this is Jordy. *He* knows his way around."

Checking Details

You can reread a text to check details you may not have noticed or remembered the first time. This helps you to understand what you have read.

1. Reread "Collections Galore" to check for details.
2. Write **yes** on the line if the details in the sentence are correct.
3. If they are not correct, draw a line through the word that is wrong and write the correct word on the line.

Examples: Andrew started his collection ~~six~~ years ago. <u>four</u>

It started when his mom gave him one as a present. <u>yes</u>

1. Andrew often makes his figures do handstands and flips. _____

2. Some of Kaitlin's pennies were collected by her great grandfather. _____

3. She is trying to have a penny for every year in her album. _____

4. Britney's dad bought her pet hamster in a pet store. _____

5. Stephanie has a rock magnet from the Grand Canyon. _____

How Did I Do?

Check your answers with those on page 97 and fill in the chart on page 100.

More to Do

Think of a collection that you have, or that a friend has. Write 4 sentences to tell what kind of collection it is, how it got started, and 2 interesting details about it.

My Self-Check

I have 4 sentences. . . . . ❑

I explained how my collection got started. . . . . ❑

I described 2 interesting details about my collection. . . . . ❑

Reading for Meaning

Authors use words to give you a certain "picture." You may need to think carefully about the meaning of some words to really understand what the author is saying.

1. Reread "Our Home Is the Sea" to find the sentences below.
2. Change the underlined word to the one that is closest in meaning.
3. Rewrite the sentence.

Example: I am the <u>eldest</u> son. (only, oldest, odd)
   <u>I am the oldest son.</u>

1. I <u>stuff</u> my report card into a pocket. (crash, cram, fold)

_____

2. A mother with a baby <u>strapped</u> on her back bends down. (tied, tucked, lying)

_____

3. I <u>hurry</u> down the stairs and get off. (hop, jump, rush)

_____

4. As <u>quietly</u> as I can, I walk past the old man. (quickly, noiselessly, bravely)

_____

5. The night mist falls <u>gently</u> down as we eat. (softly, suddenly, heavily)

_____

How Did I Do?
Check your answers with those on page 97 and fill in the chart on page 100.

More to Do
Write 2 or more words that mean the same as
1. quickly
2. spread
Check the dictionary meaning of your 2 words.

My Self-Check
I wrote 2 words for **quickly.** . . . . ❑
I wrote 2 words for **spread.** . . . . ❑
I checked the dictionary meanings. . . . . ❑

Understanding Characters

You can learn about characters' feelings and thoughts by reading carefully what they do and say. This will help you to guess what they might do.

1. Reread "Brothers and Sisters."

2. Complete the sentences by choosing the character that matches the information.

Ben	Trey	Juanita	Valerie	Maura	Steven

Example: Ben doesn't like his mom spending so much time with the baby.

1. _____ gets tired of hearing everyone say the baby is cute.

2. _____'s big sister is like another mom.

3. _____'s big brother often calls him a pest.

4. _____ feels her sister understands more than anyone else how she feels.

5. Sometimes _____'s sister acts so grown-up she can't talk to her.

3. Write the word that best describes how the character might feel about the information.

Example: Ben might feel <u>lonely</u> . (excited, happy, lonely)

6. Valerie might feel _____ . (happy, jealous, safe)

7. Steven might feel _____ . (angry, safe, upset)

8. Maura might feel _____ . (lonely, happy, jealous)

9. Juanita might feel _____ . (upset, proud, lonely)

10. Trey might feel _____ . (worried, proud, happy)

How Did I Do?

Check your answers with those on page 98 and fill in the chart on page 100.

Following Story Events

You need to think about story events, and the order in which they took place, to understand how the problem in a story is solved.

1. Reread "Roses for Gita."

2. Number the story events to show the correct order.

1	*Example:* Gita made wind chimes.
	Gita put the chimes in Mr. Flinch's mailbox.
	Gita wandered outside to look at the hole she had dug.
	Gita heard a soft tinkling sound.
	Gita asked Mr. Flinch to help her plant the First Rose.
	Mr. Flinch asked Gita to help him hang the chimes.
	Mr. Flinch growled at Gita.
	Mr. Flinch gave Gita a bouquet of roses.
	Gita saw Mr. Flinch playing the violin.
	Gita looked over the fence at her neighbour's garden.

3. Which event helped most to solve the problem? _____

_____

How Did I Do?

Check your answers with those on page 98 and fill in the chart on page 100.

More to Do

Write what you think the problem was in this story.
Describe another way the problem could have been solved.

My Self-Check

I described the problem. . . . . ☐
I described another way to solve the problem. . . . . ☐

To accompany "Roses for Gita"

Listing Facts to Compare

You can check facts by rereading and looking carefully at illustrations. When you list the facts, it is easy to compare how things are the same and how they are different.

1. Reread the poem "two friends" and study the illustration.
2. Use the chart to show how the two friends are the same and how they are different.

Lydia	Shirley
– has three pigtails	*Example:* – has two pigtails
– has blue sneakers	–
– has a necklace	–
– has a yellow beret	–
– has stripes across on pants	–
– has buttons on her shirt	–
– has black hair	–
– has brown eyes	–
– has a red collar	–
– doesn't have pierced ears	–
– has a friend	–

How Did I Do?

Check your answers with those on page 98 and fill in the chart on page 100.

More to Do

Make a picture of you with your friend. Show 2 ways that you are alike and 2 ways that you are different.

My Self-Check

I have 2 people in my picture. . . . . ❑
I have 2 likenesses. . . . . ❑
I have 2 differences. . . . . ❑

To accompany "two friends"

Reading New Words

You will meet words that are new to you when you read. You can try a new word in the sentence to see if it makes sense.

1. Find the words in the list below in "Ivan and the All-Stars."

2. Choose a word that makes sense to complete each sentence.

unpacking	repeated	cobwebs	distance	scuffing	regular
peppermint	actually	famous	firmly	blanket	

Example: "No, you cannot stay up to watch the baseball game," Mom said <u>firmly.</u>

1. In the new house, Ivan had to help mom with the _____ .

2. Twice the lady _____ that she couldn't help Ivan become a star.

3. Spiders had left many _____ in Ivan's garage.

4. Stretch, the cat, liked to curl up on a soft _____ to watch the game.

5. "You have been _____ up dirt again! Your shoes are dusty," said Ivan's mom.

6. The cat stayed a good _____ away from home plate to be safe from the ball.

7. Everyone knows the names of the _____ movie stars.

8. The lady at the desk liked to eat _____ candy.

9. Ivan had never _____ played baseball before.

10. When Ivan joined they had enough players for a _____ team.

How Did I Do?
Check your answers with those on page 98 and fill in the chart on page 100.

To accompany "Ivan and the All-Stars"

Following a Recipe

It is important to read a recipe carefully before you begin cooking, so that you know what you need to get ready and understand the steps you have to follow.

1. Read the recipe for Soda Bread.
2. Answer the questions below.

Example: How many ingredients will you need?
   <u>I will need 7 ingredients.</u>

1. What kind of bowls will you need?

   _____

2. What will you do first, when you have the ingredients and utensils ready?

   _____

3. What temperature will you use to bake the bread? _____

4. Which ingredients will you sift?

   _____

5. Which utensil will you use to mix the dry ingredients?

   _____

6. What do you need to do with the egg after you break the shell?

   _____

7. How much buttermilk will you add to the milk?

   _____

8. Where will you put the dough?

   _____

9. How long will it take to cook the loaf? _____

10. How will you know when it is cooked?

   _____

How Did I Do?

Check your answers with those on page 99 and fill in the chart on page 100.

To accompany "Billy's World"

Soda Bread

What You Need:

Ingredients	Utensils
Dry Ingredients 750 mL flour 10 mL sugar 5 mL baking soda 5 mL baking powder **Wet Ingredients** 1 egg 325 mL buttermilk	large bowl small bowl metric measuring cup sifter metric measuring spoons wooden spoon fork non-stick loaf pan

What You Do:

1. Preheat oven to 180°C.
2. Sift the first 4 ingredients into large bowl.
3. Mix well.
4. Beat egg in small bowl.
5. Add buttermilk to beaten egg.
6. Make a hole in centre of dry mixture.
7. Pour wet mixture into dry mixture.
8. Stir until dough is formed.
9. Spread dough into loaf pan.
10. Bake at 180°C for 1 hour, or until golden brown on top.

To accompany "Billy's World"

Finding the Cause

When you read, think about how one or more events can make other events happen. This helps you to understand why a story might end in a certain way.

1. Read "The Tale of a Lost Nail."
2. Think about how one event caused others to happen.
3. Write the events in order below.

Events

When the miller returned the horse and cart were gone.
The horse's shoe was loose.
The miller lost everything.
The miller left his horse and cart to look for the shoe.
The horse lost a nail from its shoe.
The horse's shoe came off.

Example: <u>The horse lost a nail from its shoe.</u>   SO⟶

1. _____   SO⟶

2. _____   SO⟶

3. _____   SO⟶

4. _____   SO⟶

5. _____

How Did I Do?

Check your answers with those on page 99 and fill in the chart on page 100.

To accompany "The Day They Saved Her Majesty"

The Tale of a Lost Nail

There was once a lazy miller who had many bags of flour piled in his mill. There was scarcely room for one more. Finally he decided he could laze no longer and would have to take his flour to the market. He piled the bags of flour in his cart and hitched the cart to his only horse. As he was about to move off, he noticed his horse had a loose shoe. When he examined the shoe, he saw that there was a nail missing.

"Oh, dear!" said the miller. "I should take my horse to the blacksmith to have it fixed, but it's such a long way. I have only the energy to go to the market today. I'm sure one missing nail won't matter."

So he jumped into his cart, pulled on the reins, and drove off to market.

When he had travelled some distance, the horse slowed down. The miller tugged on the reins. The horse slowed down even more, so the miller got out of the cart to examine his horse's hoof again. The shoe was gone!

"Oh, dear, now I will have to go back and search for that shoe."

He left the horse and cart and the bags of flour under the trees, and told his horse to wait until he returned with the shoe.

The miller walked slowly, looking carefully along the path for the missing horseshoe. He didn't notice a stranger who was strolling along on the other side.

After much searching, the miller was back at the mill and still hadn't found the shoe. "I must have missed it somehow," he said. "I will just have to retrace my steps and have a better look."

Wearily, he trudged back along the road, his head down, looking for the shoe all the way. Not a sign of it anywhere! Finally he reached the spot where he had left his horse. Both horse and cart were gone!

He searched and searched until the sun went down, but no horse and cart. At last he gave up and returned home. To this day he's still looking for them!

To accompany "The Day They Saved Her Majesty"

Checking the Meaning

When you read you will sometimes meet words you don't know the meaning of. You can
- ➤ decide what you think the word means
- ➤ reread the sentence or read on to get more information

1. Reread "Hoot Club Super-Projects" to find the words listed in the first column.
2. For each word, choose the meaning that best fits in "Hoot Club Super-Projects."
3. Write the best meaning in the second column.

Word	The Meaning I Chose
Example: reduce	lessen
1. preserve (page 53)	
2. transplanted (page 54)	
3. patience (page 55)	
4. challenged (page 55)	
5. invading (page 56)	

	Meaning One	Meaning Two
reduce	lessen	diet
preserve	keep alive	prepare by boiling water
transplanted	moved to another place	replaced a body organ with another
patience	a card game played by one person	ability to wait calmly
challenged	questioned	invited to participate
invading	swarming into	infesting (or taking over)

How Did I Do?

Check your answers with those on page 99 and fill in the chart on page 100.

More to Do

Choose 2 other words from the selection that have more than one meaning. Write 2 different meanings for each word.

My Self-Check

I chose 2 other words. . . . .❑

I wrote 2 different meanings for each word. . . . .❑

Checking Information

You may need to reread a story to find the information to answer questions. This helps you to be sure you're thinking of the correct information.

1. Read each question and the 2 answers.
2. Reread "The Catfish Palace" to check the information.
3. Circle the answer that best fits the text information.

Example:

Where was the pet store?

a) It was near Cindy's house.

b) It was in the town.

1. How do you know this was a good pet store?

   a) They had plenty of fish.

   b) The cages were clean, the water was fresh, and the budgies were happy.

2. What part of the pet store made Cindy unhappy?

   a) She was unhappy that the big catfish was in such a small space.

   b) She didn't like the cement walls of the catfish tank.

3. Why did the veterinarian release the dugong?

   a) It is an endangered sea mammal.

   b) He thought the person who captured it was mistreating it.

4. What surprise did Cindy have when she went back to the pet store?

   a) The catfish had been moved to the window.

   b) The catfish tank was empty.

5. Why would the storeowner want to get another catfish?

   a) Many people came to the store to look at it.

   b) The store was called "The Catfish Palace."

How Did I Do?

Check your answers with those on page 99 and fill in the chart on page 100.

To accompany "The Catfish Palace"

Understanding Characters

You can learn about the kinds of people characters are by reading carefully what they do and say. This helps you to predict what will happen in a story.

1. Reread "The Fairy-Tale Files."
2. Use the chart to list the characters with their descriptions, and match an experience to each character.

Character(s)	Description	Experience
Example: Ananse	lazy, cunning, greedy	Title: <u>Ananse's Feast</u> This cunning character was tricked by a clever turtle.
1.		Title: _____
2.		Title: _____
3.		Title: _____
4.		Title: _____
5.		Title: _____

Experiences

She was helped by a doll.	She proved she had much to teach a strong man.
He gave the world warmth and light.	Because of his greed his clothes were ruined.
This cunning character was tricked by a clever turtle.	In return for new suits they left good luck behind.

How Did I Do?

Check your answers with those on page 101 and fill in the chart on page 107.

Reading for Meaning

Authors use words to give you a certain message. You may need to think carefully about the meaning of some words to really understand what the author is saying.

1. Reread "The Enchanted Pitcher" to locate the ideas below.
2. Change the underlined word to the one that is closest in meaning.
3. Rewrite the sentence.

Example: It was the <u>finest</u> oil he had ever tasted. (delicious, best, purest)
<u>It was the best oil he had ever tasted.</u>

1. Rachel made a <u>beautiful</u> pitcher. (lovely, excellent, perfect)

_____

2. The potter <u>sniffed</u> the oil to check if it was good. (tasted, smelled, breathed)

_____

3. They <u>discovered</u> it was the finest oil they had ever tasted. (located, found, saw)

_____

4. Rachel was <u>furious</u> when she found the imp was in the jug. (wild, frantic, mad)

_____

5. The pitcher was <u>completely</u> full with oil. (entirely, all, almost)

_____

How Did I Do?
Check your answers with those on page 101 and fill in the chart on page 107.

More to Do
Write 2 more words that mean the same as
1. hurried
2. vanished
Check the dictionary meaning of your 2 words.

My Self-Check
I wrote 2 words for **hurried**. . . . .❑
I wrote 2 words for **vanished**. . . . .❑
I checked the dictionary meanings. . . . .❑

Retelling a Story

When you retell a story, tell or write about how it began, what happened in the middle, and how it ended. You can use exact words from the text or say it in your own words.

1. Reread "The Princess and the Pea" to help you complete the story.

Example:

Once a prince was looking for a <u>real princess</u> to marry. He_____

_____ and met many princesses, but he was

never sure that _____ .

One evening _____ raged around the palace. There was

_____ and lightning and _____ .

Suddenly _____

and _____ went to open it.

Standing in front of the gate was a princess, but what a sight she was with _____

_____ !

She announced _____ .

The old queen decided she would _____

_____ . So she went into the bedroom, _____

on the bottom of the mattress, piled _____ ,

and then put _____ .

The princess _____ .

_____ , when she was asked

how she had slept, the princess answered, " _____

_____ . There must have been something hard in the bed because

_____ ."

And so they knew she was a real princess, for _____

_____ . The prince _____

_____ , and the pea was placed _____ .

How Did I Do?

Check your answers with those on page 101 and fill in the chart on page 107.

Sorting Text from a Play

The author of a play tells you which lines are character lines, which tell a character what to do, and which describe the set. You can often tell the difference by the kind of print used.

1. Reread "Mr. Frog Went A-Courtin'."
2. Use these headings to sort the following kinds of text.

Character lines	Character direction	Set description

Example:
MR. FROG: I'll ride up to Ms. Mousie's door. | Character lines |

1. *At left are woods, represented by old tree.*

2. *MS. MOUSE sits in rocking chair, sewing.*

3. UNCLE RAT: Where will the wedding supper be?

4. *(They point left.)*

5. *Meadow, near hollow tree.*

6. *MOTH enters, carrying tablecloth.*

7. BUG: Three green beans and a black-eyed pea.

8. *(Remains standing to announce other visitors)*

9. CHICK: I ate so much it made me sick.

10. *(All sing "Mr. Frog Went A-Courtin'.")*

How Did I Do?
Check your answers with those on page 102 and fill in the chart on page 107.

More to Do
Draw the setting for Scene 2, using information on page 22.
Add details of your own.

My Self-Check
In my scene:
I showed a meadow. . . . . ❑
I showed a hollow tree. . . . . ❑
I added my own details. . . . . ❑

Finding Information

When you read, you can find some of the information right there in the story. You may have to guess some other information from clues that the author gives you.

1. Read "Small Yet Sure."
2. Write **S** beside statements about information that was **in the story**. Write **G** beside information that you **guessed** from author clues.

Example: The family was going to drive to Grandma's.	G
1. Mom was baking a birthday cake.	
2. First Kwan volunteered to go on the errand.	
3. Grandma liked to read the Saturday newspaper.	
4. Mom needed flour, candles, and a newspaper.	
5. Loc thought he could remember better than anyone else in the family.	
6. Nikki took more time to go to the store than her brothers did.	
7. Loc could only remember one item on the list.	
8. Kwan and Loc thought Nikki would not be able to do the errand.	
9. Nikki entered the store saying "Flour, candles, newspaper."	
10. Mom was proud of Nikki.	

How Did I Do?

Check your answers with those on page 102 and fill in the chart on page 107.

More to Do

Choose one statement you guessed and write the clue from the story that proves this information.

My Self-Check

I chose one statement I guessed. . . . .☐
I wrote the clue(s) from the story. . . . .☐

To accompany "The Name of the Tree"

Small Yet Sure

One Saturday morning Mom was busy baking a cake to take to Grandma's. Loc and Kwan were busy washing the car. Their small sister, Nikki, was busy telling her stuffed animals she'd have to leave them alone overnight.

"Oh, dear! I don't have enough flour. Who will go to the store?" asked Mom.

At once Kwan volunteered. "I'll go. I'm the fastest runner around here."

"Great!" said Mom. "And please pick up some birthday candles and the newspaper for grandma."

"No problem!" answered Kwan, and off he ran.

At the corner he met his friend Toni with her new bike. When Toni suggested Kwan try it out, he asked if he could ride it home to show Loc. Minutes later Kwan was pedalling up his own driveway. Mom met him at the door.

"That was quick," she said. "But where are the flour, candles, and paper?"

Kwan looked at his mom in dismay and told her he hadn't gone to the store yet.

Immediately Loc suggested that he should go since he had the best memory. Kwan felt a little foolish and told Toni he would have to get back to his car washing.

Loc dashed straight to the store. Inside, he looked at the shelves, and then at Mr. Tenaka.

"I know Mom needed flour, but I forget what else."

Back home he went. Mom met him at the door. "That was quick," she said. "But where are the flour, candles, and paper?"

"Oh, mom, I could only remember the flour and came home to check what else."

"Can no one around here do this simple errand?" asked Mom.

Nikki said she could. Kwan said she was much too small, and Loc said she was far too slow. Mom said, "Can you remember?"

"Oh, yes. Flour, candles, and the newspaper," replied Nikki.

Kwan shook his head and Loc mumbled as off Nikki went, saying to herself, "Flour, candles, newspaper, flour, candles, newspaper." All the way around the corner she repeated the list. When she entered the store she was still saying, "Flour, candles, newspaper."

Mr. Tenaka reached for the three items and placed them in a bag. Holding it tightly, Nikki walked home. Mom met her at the door. She looked in the bag. "Flour, candles, newspaper," she said, smiling. "That's my girl. You may be small but I can be sure *you'll* remember."

Kwan and Loc both admitted, "She wasn't so slow, either."

To accompany "The Name of the Tree"

Reading New Words

You will meet new words when you read. You can
- ➤ try a word that makes sense
- ➤ break the word into parts you know

1. Reread "Cinderella Around the World" to find the words in the box below.
2. Complete each sentence with one of the words.
3. Show how you can break each word into parts.

Example: The Rough-Face Girl is treated <u>cruelly</u>.

[<u>cru</u> – <u>el</u> – <u>ly</u>]

object	enchantment	adventures	invisible
mistreated	festival	Algonquin	kimono
cruelly	nobleman	delighted	

1. Cinderella was warned that the _____ would end at midnight.

[_____ – _____ – _____]

2. A ghost is an _____ being.

[_____ – _____ – ___ – _____]

3. Her stepsisters _____ Cinderella.

[_____ – _____ – ___]

4. The Nigerian story tells that Cinderella went to a dance _____.

[_____ – _____ – _____]

5. The slipper was the _____ that helped the prince to find Cinderella.

[_____ – _____]

6. The Japanese Cinderella wore a beautiful _____.

[_____ – _____ – _____]

7. The _____ Peoples call their Cinderella "Rough-Face Girl."

[_____ – _____ – _____]

8. A _____ married Benizara.

[_____ – _____ – _____]

9. Billy Beg, the son of an Irish king, had many exciting _____.

[_____ – ____ – _____]

10. The clever poem Benizara wrote _____ the nobleman

[_____ – _____ – _____]

How Did I Do?
Check your answers with those on page 102 and fill in the chart on page 107.

To accompany "Cinderella Around the World"

Interpreting Poem Ideas

Authors of poems often write ideas in ways that are different from the way they would write a story or a report. They may leave words out, add capitals, and write sentences in an unusual order.

1. The sentences in the first column are written as you would find them in a story or report. Find lines in "The Hare and the Tortoise" that mean the same as each of these sentences.

Example: The hare told the tortoise he was too slow to go anywhere.	Called the hare. "You no-go-poke Anywhere."
1. The tortoise was sure he could beat the hare.	
2. The two animals built a track in the shape of an egg.	
3. After he ran part of the race, the hare went to sleep.	
4. Tortoise passed Hare as he slept.	
5. By taking a nap the hare lost the race.	

How Did I Do?

Check your answers with those on page 103 and fill in the chart on page 107.

Diagramming Story Plot

In some stories, the author writes a lot of events that come to a turning point. The events following the turning point bring the story to a logical end or to a conclusion.

1. Read "Humpty Dumpty."

2. Write the events that lead up to the turning point and the events that end the story.

Events

Humpty crashed and broke.	The soldiers and horses tried to fix Humpty with glue.	He leaned forward to have a better look.
The soldiers and horses tried to fix Humpty with tape.	Humpty saw a waving banner.	Humpty sat down on the wall for a rest.
The soldiers gave the basket to the king.	He lost his balance.	The soldiers picked up the pieces.
Humpty heard the soldiers and horses approach.	Humpty got tired	Humpty went for a stroll.

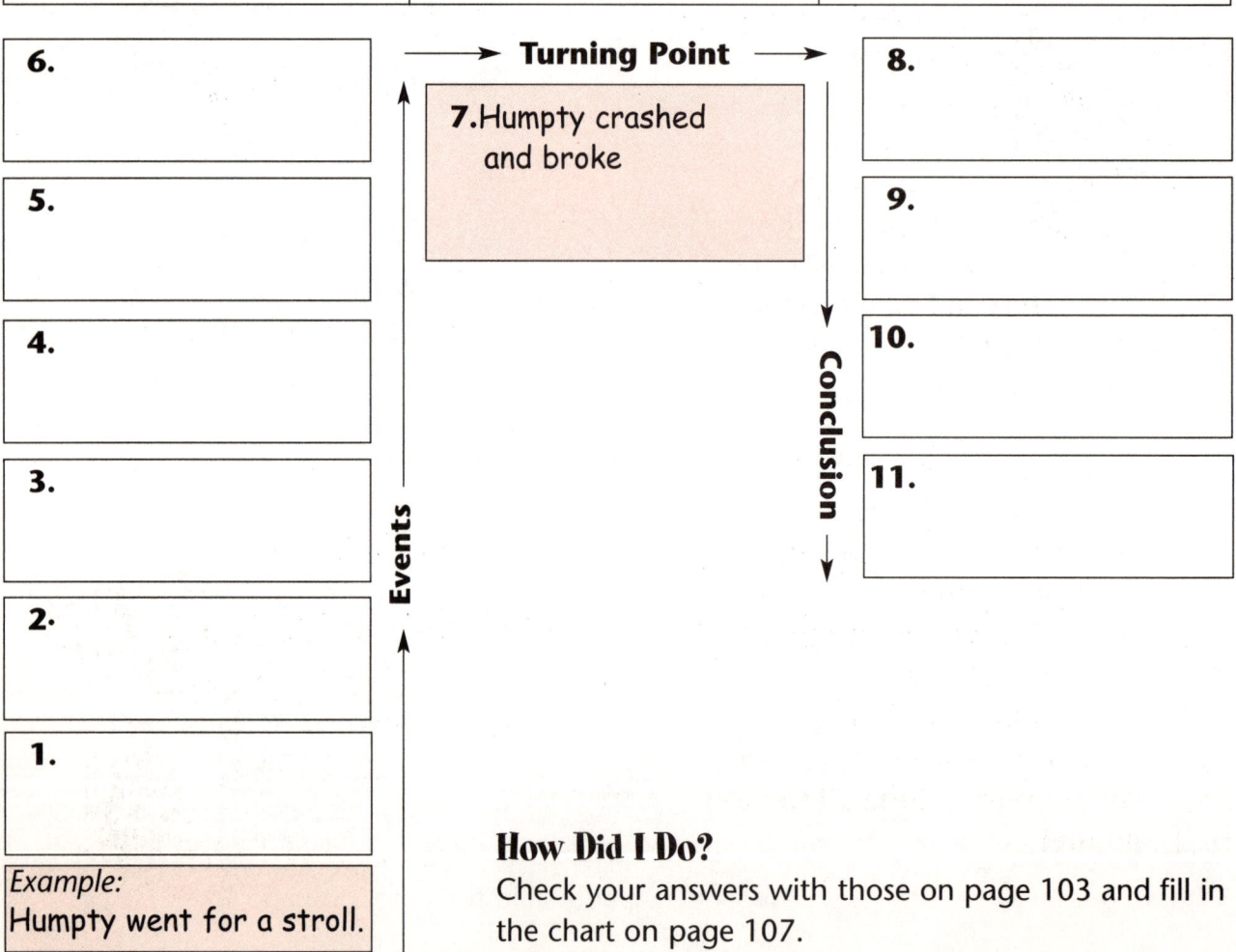

6.

5.

4.

3.

2.

1.

Example:
Humpty went for a stroll.

Events

Turning Point

7. Humpty crashed and broke

Conclusion

8.

9.

10.

11.

How Did I Do?

Check your answers with those on page 103 and fill in the chart on page 107.

To accompany "The Extraordinary Cat"

Humpty Dumpty

Once upon a time there was a little egg man called Humpty Dumpty. He was very proud of his unusual shape and his very fragile shell-like skin. Now Humpty was rather plump, especially round the middle, and when he went for a walk he would often get out of breath and have to sit down to rest.

One day he was out for a stroll near the castle where the king lived. Very soon he was breathless and his legs felt weak. He thought he had better rest a while. In front of him he spied a low part on the castle wall. Carefully he climbed on to the wall and sat down. What a relief! That round tummy was heavy to carry around.

Suddenly he heard the noise of trotting horses and a bugle sounding. Humpty knew it must be the castle soldiers out on guard duty. When he caught sight of a waving banner, he stretched forward to have a better look. He felt himself wobbling and tried to grasp onto one of the bricks, but down he went, rolling all the way to the ground.

Crash! All over the path there was broken shell and splattered yolk and egg white.

At that very moment the castle soldiers rode up and saw the disaster. Quickly they dismounted. Both horses and soldiers tried to put Humpty Dumpty together again. They tried tape. They tried glue. Unfortunately they couldn't make the pieces of Humpty stick together.

Sadly the castle soldiers picked up all the pieces and placed them carefully in a basket lined with straw. They laid Humpty's little suit and tall hat alongside, and they took the basket to the king.

The storyteller claims that the king of the castle still has that basket of broken eggshells today.

To accompany "The Extraordinary Cat"

Mapping a Story

You can make a pictorial map of a story you have read to help you to "picture" the story events and to see what the setting might look like.

1. Read "Chicken Licken."

2. Make a pictorial map to show at least 5 events (places where Chicken Licken went, roads she took, and friends she met).

3. Use sketches, signs, arrows, and labels on your map.

Example:

Title: _____

How Did I Do?

Check your answers with those on page 104 and fill in the chart on page 107.

Chicken Licken

One sunny morning Chicken Licken went out to collect her mail. Suddenly an acorn dropped from the nearby oak tree and hit her on the head. She looked up. "Oh, dear," she cried, "the sky is falling down! I must go and tell the king."

She packed a light lunch, locked up her house, and set off through Sherwood Forest to the king's palace. At the clump of pine trees she met Ducky Lucky.

"Where are you off to?" asked Ducky Lucky. When Chicken Licken told her that she had felt the sky falling and was going to tell the king, Ducky Lucky decided she would go along too.

The two friends came out of the forest and walked along the river bank. As they crossed over London Bridge they bumped into Gander Dander.

"Where are you two ladies off to on such a beautiful morning?" he inquired. When Chicken Licken explained the problem and that they were going to inform the king, Gander Dander thought he might as well join them on their trip.

Happy to be together, the three of them strolled to Muffet Meadow, where they rested under the big apple tree and shared Chicken Licken's lunch. Soon they moved on, and as they passed Floss Mill, who should they come upon but Foxy Loxy!

"Now where are you all going to on this fine day?" he asked.

"Well," replied Gander Dander, "Chicken Licken is going to let the king know that the sky is falling, and we are tagging along with her."

"Do you know where the king's palace is? I know a short cut and could take you there very fast," said Foxy Loxy slyly.

The three friends thought this a good idea and agreed that Foxy Loxy should lead the way. They followed him into Willows Wood, along the narrow path. Soon they came to a thick clump of bushes. Foxy Loxy explained that a tunnel through the bushes would lead right to the palace gate. He cleverly stood aside to let his fowl friends enter and he followed them into the darkness.

Chicken Licken, Ducky Lucky, and Gander Dander were never seen or heard of again. And no one told the king that the sky was falling.

It was reported, though, that Foxy Loxy had grown to be quite plump.

To accompany "Mother Holle"

Finding Proof of Characteristics

You can find proof of the characteristics of the characters in a story by reading carefully what they do and say.

1. Reread "How Eagle Got His Good Eyes."
2. Read the sentences in the first column.
3. Choose the proof that proves each characteristic. Write the proof in the second column.

Characteristic	Proof
Example: Eagle was <u>generous</u>.	He shared his fish with Nanabush.
1. Nanabush was <u>clever</u>.	**a)** **b)**
2. Eagle was <u>trusting</u>.	
3. Manitou was <u>kind</u>.	**a)** **b)**

Proofs

He shared his fish with Nanabush.	He set a trap for Eagle.
He agreed to make a deal with Nanabush.	He used lightning to give Eagle eyesight.
He burned the net that trapped Eagle.	He gave Eagle the eyes of the dead fish.

How Did You Do?

Check your answers with those on page 104 and fill in the chart on page 107.

Sequencing Events

Authors usually write one event to follow another in a story. To understand the storyline, it is important to think about the events in the order that they happened.

1. Reread "The Lad Who Went to the North Wind."
2. Number the events to show how one action followed another. Some events have been marked to help you.

1	*Example*: The North Wind blew away the lad's oatmeal three times.
	The North Wind gave the lad a magic cloth that could serve dinner.
	The landlady stole the cloth and replaced it with an ordinary cloth.
	The lad went to see the North Wind a second time.
	The North Wind gave him a stick that could beat when it was told to.
5	The lad took the cloth home to his mother but it wouldn't serve dinner.
13	The lad told the stick to lay on and it beat the landlord.
	The landlord gave the magic cloth and the goat back to the lad.
	The lad told the stick to stop.
	The lad went home with the North Wind's three gifts.
2	The lad went to see the North Wind.
	The lad took the goat home to his mother but it wouldn't make coins.
7	The North Wind gave the lad a goat that could make golden coins.
10	The lad went to see the North Wind a third time.
	The landlord tried to steal the stick.
	The landlord stole the goat and replaced it with an ordinary goat.

How Did I Do?
Check your answers with those on page 104 and fill in the chart on page 107.

Checking Word Choice

You will meet new words as you read. You can
- ➤ think of a word that makes sense and sounds right
- ➤ check your choice by looking at the beginning and ending letters

1. Reread "The Finding Princess" to find the words that are underlined.
2. Replace the word with one that means the same and begins and ends with the given letters.
3. Think of the word **before** you check in a dictionary.

Example: She breakfasted on wild berries <u>gathered</u> from the woods. [**c**o̲l̲l̲e̲c̲t**ed**]

1. The princess set out to find for herself what she <u>required</u>. [**n** _ _ _ **ed**]

2. "I have found my cup of pearl!" <u>declared</u> the princess. [**st** _ _ **ed**]

3. The grandmother brought shoes <u>embroidered</u> by ladies-in-waiting. [**s** _ _ **ed**]

4. The grandfather brought a bird <u>adorned</u> by craftsmen. [**d** _ _ _ _ _ _ **ed**]

5. "We have tried but we can't make you happy," said the <u>grown-ups</u>. [**a** _ _ _ _ _ **s**]

6. The princess found a shell worn by the sea and <u>lustrous</u>. [**sh** _ _ **y**]

7. She saw the moon surrounded by a soft, glowing <u>circle</u> of light. [**r** _ _ **g**]

8. She came upon a <u>meadow</u> where children were dancing. [**f** _ _ _ **d**]

9. The princess <u>scattered</u> the crumbs in the grass. [**th** _ _ **w**]

10. They found the princess's boots <u>right</u> where she left them. [**ex** _ _ _ **ly**]

How Did I Do?
Check your answers with those on page 105 and fill in the chart on page 107.

More to Do
Choose 2 other sentences from the story where a word could be replaced by another with the same meaning.
Give the beginning and ending letter clues.

My Self-Check
I wrote 2 sentences from the story where a word could be
replaced by another with the same meaning. . . . . ❑
I wrote the beginning and ending letter clues. . . . . ❑

Recognizing What Is the Same and What Is Different

Organizing information on a chart will help you to quickly see what is the same and what is different between information.

1. Reread "Bend a Wire."
2. Read the rhyme "Pat-a-Cake."
3. Use the chart to show the differences in the ideas of these 2 rhymes.

Pat-a-Cake

Pat-a-cake, pat-a-cake,
Baker's man.
Bake me a cake
Fast as you can.
Roll it and pat it
And mark it with "B,"
And put it in the oven
For Baby and me.

My Comparison Chart of 2 Rhymes		
Title	**Bend a Wire**	**Pat-a-Cake**
Worker		
Material Used	*Example:* wire	*Example:* material not included
Actions of the Worker	*Example:* bending **1.** **2.**	*Example:* rolling
What Worker Made		
What Worker Added	*Example:* a charm	*Example:* a "B" mark
Who the Worker Made It For		**1.** **2.**

How Did I Do?

Check your answers with those on page 105 and fill in the chart on page 107.

More to Do

Write 2 ways in which the rhymes are alike.

My Self-Check

I wrote 2 ways the rhymes are alike. . . . . ❑

To accompany "African Mother Goose Rhymes"

Analyzing a Story

You can get a clear picture of the plot when you read a story by thinking about the setting, the characters, the events, the problem, and the solution.

1. Reread "The Other Frog Prince."

2. Use the chart to identify the story parts.

SETTING

TITLE
"The Other Frog Prince"

AUTHOR
Jon Scieszka

CHARACTERS
1.
2.

PROBLEM

SOLUTION

EVENTS
Example: Princess sits by the pond.
1.
2.
3.
4.
5.

How Did I Do?

Check your answers with those on page 105 and fill in the chart on page 107.

More to Do

Write a new title for "The Other Frog Prince." Explain why you think your title is better than Jon Scieszka's.

My Self-Check

I wrote a new title. . . . . ❏

I explained why I think it is a better one. . . . . ❏

Using Antonyms Meaningfully

Antonyms are words that are opposite in meaning.

1. Reread "New Tales from Old" to find the bolded words in the sentences.

2. Write the opposite of the bolded word above it.

3. Write **yes** or **no** to decide if the new sentence makes sense in this article.

Example: <u> erases </u> A technician then **records** the voices, sound effects, and music.	no
1. Every good film **begins** with a good story idea.	
2. We would decide how **long** Red Riding Hood's hair will be.	
3. I then help **hire** the actors who give the characters their voices.	
4. The actors read the script **aloud** together.	
5. The artists would draw where Red Riding Hood and the wolf are to be placed when they meet in the woods for the **first** time.	
6. The animators create **many** drawings of each character's actions.	
7. The sets of drawings are checked to make sure the movement is **clear**.	
8. **After** the drawings are painted, they are filmed onto video tape.	
9. It takes **over** six months to make Red Riding Hood into a half-hour cartoon.	
10. It sounds like a lot of **hard** work, and it is.	

How Did I Do?

Check your answers with those on page 106 and fill in the chart on page 107.

Classifying Information

When you use a chart to classify (group) information you have read, it lets you see all the facts in one place. Then you can see what is the same and different in the text.

1. Reread "Coral: At Home on a Reef" to look for information in the text and photographs.
2. Use the chart headings to classify the facts below.

Facts About Creatures

– triplefin	– file shell	– octopus	– butterfly fish
– red – long white tentacles	– pinkish-red – sucker-covered arms	– yellow and black – long pointy snout – tiny mouth	– orange – glowing stripes
– floating food	– tiny sea creatures	– coral polyps	– crabs
– attaches to reef with its sticky threads	– uses reef as a "lookout tower"	– plucks polyps with nose	– uses arms to grab prey
– coral reef	– coral reef	– coral reef	– coral reef

Classifying Creatures

Animal	Appearance	Home	Food	Habits
Example: – file shell	– red – long white tentacles	– coral reef	– floating food	– attaches to reef with its sticky threads

How Did I Do?

Check your answers with those on page 108 and fill in the chart on page 112.

Reading Author Clues

When you read, you will find that the author doesn't always give you all the information right in the text. Sometimes the author will just give clues to suggest information.

1. Reread "Worm Ways and Ant Antics."

2. Read the sentences and write the clues that the author gave in the text.

Example: You can find worms in Canada. (page 10)
<u>Earthworms live in countries all over the world.</u>

1. Worms are boneless creatures with few senses. (page 10)

_____

2. Worms like nighttime. (page 11) _____

3. Worms can feel vibrations. (page 11) _____

4. The worm's tiny bristles help to protect it from its enemies. (page 11)_____

_____

5. Worms find it difficult to move on smooth surfaces. (page 12)

_____

6. Ants are co-operative insects. (page 13)

_____

7. The queen ant does not need to find food. (page 13)

_____

8. Ants wouldn't like to live in the Antarctic. (page 13)

_____

9. Ants cannot live in rivers and lakes. (page 13)_____

10. An ant is a very strong insect. (page 14)

_____

How Did I Do?

Check your answers with those on page 108 and fill in the chart on page 112.

Organizing Information

When you use a chart to organize information you have read, it helps you to see the information "at a glance" and to understand how the pieces fit together.

1. Read "Afraid of Its Shadow."
2. Find the information below in the text.
3. Write the information under the headings of the organizer chart.

– in underground burrows in flat empty fields	– for about 5–6 months
– Groundhog	– wakes up every 7–10 days
– so frightened by seeing shadow it goes back to sleep for 6 more weeks	– may eat from food store
	– a shy animal
– comes out on Feb. 2 to check shadow	– mid-fall
– body temperature rises at times	"Afraid of Its Shadow"

Topic: _____

Title and how it fits:

_____

Example: – a shy animal
(1 more point)

_____

_____

When it hibernates: (2 points)

_____

_____

Where it hibernates: (1 point)

_____

_____

What happens during hibernation: (4 points)

_____

_____

_____

_____

How Did I Do?

Check your answers with those on page 108 and fill in the chart on page 112.

To accompany "The Big Sleep"

Afraid of Its Shadow

Perhaps the most famous hibernating animal in Canada is the groundhog. Some people think that a groundhog can tell us when winter will end. On February 2 in Wiarton, Ontario, people carefully watch the entrance to a groundhog's burrow to see the groundhog come out. They believe that if the groundhog comes out of its winter home and sees its shadow, it will be so scared that it will go back to sleep for six more weeks. They see this as a sign that winter will continue for 6 weeks longer.

During the late summer and fall, this shy little animal prepares for its long hibernation by eating lots of leafy plants, seeds, and nuts. These foods help to greatly increase the animal's body fat. The groundhog also collects food to store in its burrow to eat during the long winter.

A groundhog digs a long, deep burrow, often in a flat empty field. It lines the sleeping area of its burrow with hay and dried leaves.

A groundhog may begin its hibernation in September or October. It knows it is time to hibernate when its body temperature drops as the colder weather arrives. Its body temperature drops so low that the animal can no longer move and has to go to sleep.

A groundhog does not sleep continually from fall until early February, but wakes up every 7 to 10 days, when its body warms up enough. The groundhog may wake up, but it doesn't leave its burrow until about February 2. Just in time to check its shadow.

To accompany "The Big Sleep"

Reading for Meaning

Authors use words to give you a certain "picture." You may need to think carefully about the meaning of some words so that you can understand what the author is saying.

1. Reread "Katie's Letter" to find the sentences below.
2. Change the underlined word to the one that is closest in meaning. Rewrite the sentence.
3. Check your meaning in a dictionary.

Example: Katie's mother gave an <u>unhappy</u> nod. (sad, miserable, worried)
<u>Katie's mother gave a sad nod.</u>

1. Curt scratched his beard and <u>grinned</u>. (laughed, smiled, giggled)

_____

2. Curt came by to <u>view</u> the damage. (repair, find, observe)

_____

3. He'd <u>tunnelled</u> deeper than Curt had dug. (drilled, burrowed, shovelled)

_____

4. She'd tell the woodchuck he was <u>smart</u> to get the broccoli out of the trap. (good, clever, neat) _____

_____

5. She could see his black, <u>curved</u> nails. (crooked, pointed, bent)

_____

How Did I Do?

Check your answers with those on page 109 and fill in the chart on page 112.

More to Do
Write 2 or more words that mean the same as
1. careless
2. peered
Check the dictionary meaning of your 2 words.

My Self-Check
I wrote 2 words for **careless.** . . . . ❑
I wrote 2 words for **peered**. . . . . ❑
I checked the dictionary meanings. . . . . ❑

To accompany "Katie's Letter"

Interpreting Poem Ideas

An author of a poem often writes ideas in a very descriptive way. The author might leave out words, turn around sentences, and break up ideas into more than one line of text.

1. Reread "Tree Coming Up" to find the poem idea to match each of the sentences.

2. Write the poem ideas in the second column.

Part A

Example: As it grows, the shoot passes a worm in its underground home.	By a worm at home in a tunnel bed,
The shoot pokes through the rich brown soil.	
The oak shoot pushes, stretches, and pokes upwards.	
The shoot grows up past ant and beetle nests.	
It grows leaves. A tree is born!	
A green shoot breaks through an acorn seed.	

Part B

3. Write the "plain" sentences in the same order as in the poem.

Example: <u>A green shoot breaks through an acorn seed.</u>

1. _____

2. _____

3. _____

4. _____

5. _____

How Did I Do?

Check your answers with those on page 109 and fill in the chart on page 112.

Checking Details

Sometimes you may need to reread an article to be sure that you remember the details correctly.

1. Reread "Caves and Caverns" to check for details.

2. Write **yes** on the line if the details below are correct.

3. If they are not correct, draw a line through the word that is wrong and write the correct word on the line.

Examples: A lava cave can only be formed if a volcano erupts. <u>yes</u>

~~Millions~~ of caves and caverns exist in many parts of the world. <u>Thousands</u>

1. Caves sometimes begin from the depths of the land and extend downward.

   _____

2. Ice caves are formed by streams that erode tunnels under mountain glaciers.

   _____

3. The most unusual type of cave is a limestone or solution cave.

   _____

4. The ceiling crystals build up to form stone icicles called stalagmites.

   _____

5. The different colours of the stalactites are the result of changes in the minerals.

   _____

How Did I Do?

Check your answers with those on page 109 and fill in the chart on page 112.

> ## More to Do
> Use the information in "Caves and Caverns" to help you write 2 true facts and 2 false facts.
>
> ## My Self-Check
> I wrote 2 true facts. . . . .☐
> I wrote 2 false facts. . . . .☐

Reading to Remember

It's helpful to try to remember the exact words the author has used in a story you've read. This can help you to retell the story.

1. Reread "The Volcano." Try to remember the words the author uses.
2. Read the following sentences. Think of the word the author used.
3. Check in the story to see if you're correct.

Example: On the island there are lots of colorful trees and many kinds of <u>animals</u>.

1. Now for as long as anyone can remember everything has been calm and

   _____ on the island.

2. Brok hated everything on the island, but most of all he hated the _____ .

3. After many years of wearing away the rocks, the _____ finally reached the fiery centre of the volcano.

4. The whole island was _____ to pieces, and even Brok was sent flying through the air.

5. At last, when everything had calmed down, the _____ saw that the island had changed completely.

6. _____ the waterfall, there was now a beautiful lake, where the pelicans could fish in peace.

7. The volcano too was quiet, and the turtles admired its reflection in the lake as they

   _____ slowly amongst the stones.

8. Brok the troublemaker had been _____ by the volcano onto the top of a tall tree.

9. A bird took the crab from the tree, thinking he'd make a good _____ .

10. I'd like to go to that island one day and see the beautiful lake with its pelicans, and

    the mountain that was once a _____ .

How Did I Do?
Check your answers with those on page 110 and fill in the chart on page 112.

Finding Information

Sometimes you may need to reread parts of an article to be sure that you remember the facts correctly. To do this, skim the material to look for headings and key words that will help you find the right part. Then read carefully to find the information.

1. Read each sentence below.
2. Reread "Building Tunnels" to see if the information is in the article. Circle **Y** (yes) if it is. Circle **N** (no) if it isn't.

Example: The Alps are in Switzerland.   Y   Ⓝ

1. Tunnels are built in many shapes and sizes.   Y   N

2. Before building a tunnel, engineers have to plan.   Y   N

3. People have been building tunnels for a long time.   Y   N

4. To make King Hezekiah's tunnel, some diggers started at one end and some diggers started at the other end and they met in the middle.   Y   N

5. The longest tunnel ever built was King Hezekiah's tunnel.   Y   N

6. A problem when you are digging through earth or sand is to keep the hole from caving in.   Y   N

7. Tunnels are usually built to make transportation easier.   Y   N

8. The Simplon Tunnel started in Switzerland.   Y   N

9. A tunnel-building machine can be used to tunnel through rock.   Y   N

10. Soil and rock samples help engineers to decide how to build a tunnel.   Y   N

How Did I Do?

Check your answers with those on page 110 and fill in the chart on page 112.

More to Do

Do some research to find some interesting information about tunnels that wasn't in the article. Write a sentence about the information.

My Self-Check

I did some research to find interesting information
about tunnels that wasn't in the article. ....❑
I wrote a sentence about the information. ....❑

Putting Ideas in the Correct Order

You need to remember the order (sequence) in which story events take place so it makes sense and so you can retell the story to others.

1. Reread "Jonathan Cleaned Up—Then He Heard a Sound."

2. Number the events to show the correct order.

1	*Example:* Jonathan's mother went to get a can of noodles.
	All kinds of people came out of the wall, ran around the apartment, and went out the front door.
	Jonathan told his mother, "There will be no more subways here."
	Jonathan went to the jam store and carried four cases of blackberry jam back to the old man at City Hall.
	Jonathan heard a sound coming from behind the wall.
	Jonathan's mother heard a sound coming from behind the wall.
	Jonathan went to City Hall and saw the Mayor.
	Jonathan squeezed in back of the machine and saw a little old man at a very messy desk.
	Jonathan told the old man where to put the subway station.
	Jonathan's mother was still standing on the rug because she was stuck to the gum.
	On his way out of City Hall, Jonathan heard a sound.

How Did I Do?

Check your answers with those on page 110 and fill in the chart on page 112.

Identifying True Facts

You may need to reread an interview or article to help you to decide which facts are true and which are false. Read carefully to check the information.

1. Reread "Meet the Dirt Detectives!"

2. Read each of the sentences below. Print **True** if the information is true and **False** if it's not true.

3. Give the page number where you found the information.

Example: George said his mom is a teacher.   <u>False (page 58)</u>

1. This was AnnMarie's second dig.   _____

2. On this dig, George's first finds were a nail, some
   brick chips, and a piece of glass.   _____

3. AnnMarie said that she doesn't like having to go so slowly.   _____

4. It's important to check first before digging.   _____

5. The Gore Vale mansion was built in 1820.   _____

6. The dirt detectives found a marble more than eighty years
   after it was dropped.   _____

7. A trowel is a little shovel.   _____

8. A boy's club was built where family housing used to be. _____

9. In 1946, the Canadian flag was the same as the flag we fly today. _____

10. When you go on a dig, it's important to work fast.   _____

How Did I Do?

Check your answers with those on page 111 and fill in the chart on page 112.

More to Do

Use the information in "Meet the Dirt Detectives!" to help you write 2 true facts and 2 false facts.

My Self-Check

I wrote 2 true facts. . . . . ❑

I wrote 2 false facts. . . . . ❑

Matching Words and Meanings

When you meet words you don't know the meaning of, you can
- ➤ decide what meaning would make sense
- ➤ use a dictionary to check if you have the right meaning

1. Reread "Dinosaur Bones."
2. Read the meanings in the first column.
3. Write the word that matches each meaning in the second column.
4. If you are not sure, check the word in a dictionary.

Meaning	Word
Example: a large reptile that lived millions of years ago	dinosaur
1. animals that eat mainly plants	
2. a person who is trained in science	
3. having blood that stays at about the same temperature even though the temperature of the air or other surroundings change	
4. animals with long, sharp teeth and claws that eat mainly meat	
5. a display for the public	
6. having blood that changes temperature depending on the surrounding air or water	
7. the remains of an animal or plant that lived long ago	
8. a geological time period (era) known as the age of reptiles	
9. the time before history was recorded	
10. a place where stone is cut or blasted out for use in building	

cold-blooded	quarry	dinosaur	warm-blooded	herbivores	prehistoric
fossil	Mesozoic	exhibition	carnivores	scientists	

How Did I Do?

Check your answers with those on page 111 and fill in the chart on page 112.

More to Do

Choose 3 words from the second column that you like the sound of. Write a sentence using each of the words.

My Self-Check

I chose 3 words from the second column. . . . .☐
I wrote a sentence using each of the words. . . . .☐

Organizing Information in a Chart

You may find it easier to remember information if you organize it in a chart. To do this, decide on key words, then find details that give more information about each of them.

1. Reread "Discovery of Gold in the Yukon" to find the information in the first column below.
2. Decide if each piece of information is about people, places, or things.
3. Put a ✓ under the correct heading.

Organizing Information			
	People	**Places**	**Things**
Example: Dawson City		✓	
1. the greatest gold rush in history			
2. adventurers from all over the world			
3. where the Yukon and Klondike Rivers come together			
4. more than a billion dollars			
5. the frozen north			
6. steamships			
7. rubber boots, cotton goods, and hot water bottles			
8. the Yukon			
9. Belinda Mulroney			
10. the Klondike			

How Did I Do?

Check your answers with those on page 111 and fill in the chart on page 112.

More to Do
Fold a sheet of paper into 4 sections. Use crayons or markers to make pictures of 4 interesting things you know about the Klondike Gold Rush.

My Self-Check
I made 4 different pictures. . . . . ❑
Each picture tells something interesting about the Gold Rush. . . . . ❑

Discovery of Gold in the Yukon

In the late 1800s, three men set out together to search for gold. Two of the men were from the Yukon. Their names were Skookum Jim and Tagish Charlie. The third man was their American friend, George Carmack. They discovered gleaming gold in a creek and renamed the creek "Bonanza." If they discovered that same gold today, it would be worth more than a billion dollars!

Another person who went out to search for gold was Belinda Mulroney. When she arrived in the Klondike, she threw her last fifty cents (a lot of money in those days!) into the Yukon River because she was sure she'd get rich. She did get rich, but not from finding gold. Instead she started selling rubber boots, cotton goods, and hot water bottles for very high prices. Then she built a roadhouse at Bonanza Creek. By the end of the year she owned six mining properties. Soon she had enough money to pay people to build the Fairview Hotel. It was one of the most expensive buildings in Dawson City.

Soon everyone knew about the gold at Bonanza Creek. Thousands of people came to Dawson, the town that was quickly built where the Yukon and Klondike Rivers came together. One hundred thousand adventurers from all over the world set out for the frozen north. Steamships were filled with people who wanted to travel to the Yukon to find gold and get rich fast. The greatest gold rush in history was underway.

The Klondike Gold Rush was a very exciting time and many people became very rich very quickly!

To accompany "Klondike"

Comparing Ideas

Authors use many different kinds of writing to share ideas. When you compare the ideas of a poem and a report, you can see how they are the same and different. This helps you to understand the author's reason (purpose) for writing each selection.

1. Read "Far-away Mysteries" and "Our Solar System."
2. Put a ✓ under the title of the selection that has each of the ideas.
   Hint: Sometimes you will need to put a ✓ under both titles.

Comparing Ideas		
Ideas	**"Far-away Mysteries"**	**"Our Solar System"**
Example: the title tells what the selection is about		✓
1. tells about the planets		
2. makes you wonder about the planets		
3. gives facts		
4. asks a question		
5. is like a story		
6. tells you that the Sun doesn't move		
7. is fact		
8. is imaginative		
9. tells you that the planets move around the Sun		
10. names an astronomer's instrument		

How Did I Do?

Check your answers with those on page 111 and fill in the chart on page 112.

More to Do

Use the information in "Our Solar System" to help you make a picture of the planets and the Sun.

My Self-Check

There are 9 planets in my picture. . . . . ❑

The sun is in the middle. . . . . ❑

Jupiter, Saturn, Uranus, and Neptune are larger than Mercury, Earth, Venus, Mars, and Pluto. . . . . ❑

Far-away Mysteries

High, high in the sky
Far away
The planets, all in order
Make their non-stop trips around the motionless Sun.
Day after day and year after year
Never slowing down to rest for a while.

Gazing through my telescope
I wonder about all the great mysteries they hold
And if I'll ever know about their treasures . . .
And maybe their people?

Our Solar System

The solar system is made up of the Sun and nine planets. The sun sits in the middle while the planets travel around it. All the planets travel around the sun in the same direction.

The solar system is made up of two parts:

- the inner solar system, which is made up of the planets that are closest to the Sun (Mercury, Venus, Earth, and Mars), and

- the outer solar system, which is made up of the planets that are farthest from the Sun (Jupiter, Saturn, Uranus, Neptune, and Pluto).

The planets come in two sizes, small and giant.

The small planets are Mercury, Venus, Earth, Mars, and Pluto. Each of these planets is less than 13 000 km across. Mercury and Pluto are the very smallest of the small planets.

The giant planets are Jupiter, Saturn, Uranus, and Neptune.

Each of the giant planets is more than 48 000 km across. Saturn is the second largest planet and Jupiter is the largest. In fact, Jupiter is so large that you could put 1000 Earths inside it!

The giant planets are sometimes called "The Gas Giants."

Although a lot is known about the planets, there is still a lot to be learned.

Writing Questions

Thinking of questions to ask about what you're reading can help you to understand the story.

1. Read each answer below.
2. Reread "Morning on the Lake" to find the sentence that contains the answer.
3. Use the information in the sentence to make a good question for the answer.
4. Use the first word to help you to write the question. Remember to end each question with a question mark (?).

Example: a big orange ball hiding behind the trees (page 4)
What <u>is the sun?</u>

1. like a grey blanket covering the lake (page 4)
What _____

2. bare toes (page 5)
What _____

3. the centre of the lake (page 6)
Where _____

4. his steady strong arm (page 6)
What _____

5. in front of us (page 7)
Where _____

6. white squares and dots (page 7)
What _____

7. two fluffy grey babies (page 7)
What _____

8. pounding (page 8)
What _____

9. with a powerful force (page 8)
How _____

10. our story (page 8)
What _____

How Did I Do?

Check your answers with those on page 113 and fill in the chart on page 117.

Finding Proof of the Author's Feelings

Authors sometimes tell their feelings about a subject in their writing. You can find proof of the author's feelings by reading carefully and underlining the words in the selection.

1. Read "The Dandelion—A Magical Flower!"
2. Underline all the words or groups of words that prove the author thinks that the dandelion is much more than "a troublesome weed."

The Dandelion—A Magical Flower!

Have you ever thought of how magical dandelions are? When the flower turns to seeds, you can make a wish and blow the seeds off the stem. And if you blow just right and all those little seeds fly away, you just might get your wish. Magic!

And who couldn't help but love the dandelion's bright yellow colour—just like the sun! Nothing can make you feel as happy as when you're looking at a field filled with bright yellow dandelions dancing in the breeze. What a wonderful picture they make!

Best of all is that dandelions don't cost anything. Pick a bunch and you can make a beautiful bouquet for your teacher or for your home. All for free!

Most people think of the dandelion as nothing more than a troublesome weed. But I know better!

3. Copy 5 of these words or groups of words to make a list.

Example: __Magic__

1. _____

2. _____

3. _____

4. _____

5. _____

How Did I Do?

Check your answers with those on page 113 and fill in the chart on page 117.

Matching Words with Photographs

Printed words and photographs go together because they both give you information. Sometimes the words help you to understand the photographs, and sometimes the photographs help you to understand the words.

1. Reread "Seeing Through the Camera's Eye."

2. Look at the photographs and write the best words from the article to describe each picture.

Example: Photograph of the two girls (page 12)
- your neighbourhood
- to remember a special event
- a favourite place

<u>to remember a special event</u>

1. Photograph of the Dr. Martens shoes (page 13)
- flowers
- bright colours
- every face is unique

_____

2. Photograph of the boy (page 13)
- a favourite place
- every face is unique
- a collection

_____

3. Photograph of the windows (page 14)
- a portrait doesn't have to be of a person's face
- repeating patterns of reflections
- mysterious shadows

_____

4. Photograph of the butterflies (page 15)
- a collage of pictures
- repeating patterns
- a collection

_____

5. Photograph of the dog (page 16)
- an unusual pet with its owner
- your pet's unique character
- an exotic pet

_____

How Did I Do?

Check your answers with those on page 113 and fill in the chart on page 117.

Organizing Information

Organizing information in a chart can help you to see the information "at a glance" and to understand how the pieces fit together.

1. Reread "The Missing Skateboard."
2. Find the information below in the text.
3. Write the information under the headings of the organizer chart.

detective agency	missing skateboard	Angie
winning a skateboard contest	Tracy's garage	David
first day of summer vacation	long brown scratch	Prince
dog hairs	grass	Prince
jealousy	Tracy	David
around noon	the open back screen door	

Characters	**Setting** *Example:* • <u>around noon</u>	**Puzzle (Crime)**
• _____	• _____	• _____
• _____	• _____	_____
• _____	• _____	
• _____	_____	
Suspects	**Motive (Reason)**	**Clues**
• _____	• _____	• _____
• _____	• _____	• _____
	_____	• _____

Turning Point

Example: • <u>the open back screen door</u> _____

How Did I Do?

Check your answers with those on page 114 and fill in the chart on page 117.

Knowing What Happens Next

A story is made up of many events. To understand the storyline it is important to think about the events in the order they happened.

1. Reread "The Best Thing I Never Saw" and look for each of the following events.
2. Find the next thing that happened from the "What Happened Next" list and print the correct letter.

Events (What Happened)

Example:

1. Kikora's mother told her that a total solar eclipse was coming. d
2. Her mother said, "Next Tuesday is the big day." _____
3. Kikora ran to look out a window. _____
4. Her mother said, "Why don't we go out on the front porch to watch and listen for a while?" ___
5. Kikora looked around. _____
6. As Kikora watched and waited, strange things began to happen. _____
7. The cardinal ended his song. _____
8. Noonday became almost as dark as night. _____
9. Darkness lasted only a few minutes. _____
10. The cardinal once again sang his song. _____
11. Kikora's mother asked, "What did you see?" _____

What Happened Next

a) All the other birds stopped singing, too.
b) Gradually the sky lightened.
c) Kikora followed her mom outside and sat on the front steps.
d) Her mother told her about solar eclipses.
e) Kikora said, "It was the best thing I never saw!"
f) She saw nothing but clouds.
g) Kikora put a big red X on the calendar.
h) A yellow butterfly flitted among Mother's petunias.
i) Little by little the cloudy sky darkened.
j) The yellow butterfly returned to Mother's petunias.
k) The streetlight in front of Kikora's house came on.

How Did I Do?

Check your answers with those on page 114 and fill in the chart on page 117.

To accompany "The Best Thing I Never Saw"

Deciding Who, What, Why, When, Where, or How

An author gives you many different kinds of information. Some is **who** information and some of it tells **what, why, when, where,** or **how**.

1. Read the following information from "Speaking with Signs."
2. Decide if the underlined words tell you **who, what, why, when, where,** or **how**.
3. Record your answer on the line following the sentence.

Example: <u>Mrs. Woodard</u> is the teacher. <u>who</u>

1. The children are in <u>Grade 3.</u> _____

2. The children use sign language <u>because they are deaf.</u> _____

3. Deaf people sign <u>by speaking with their hands and fingers.</u> _____

4. Right after recess, the children went <u>to the drama room.</u> _____

5. The white light on the wall flashes <u>to show there's an incoming call.</u> _____

6. <u>Later in the afternoon</u>, the children watched an educational TV program.

   _____

7. <u>An interpreter</u> signs the words as the program is being filmed. _____

8. The signing appears <u>in the corner of the TV screen.</u> _____

9. Mrs. Woodard got the children's attention <u>by turning the light switch off and back on.</u> _____

10. Mrs. Bryan used <u>the sign that means "thank you".</u> _____

How Did I Do?
Check your answers with those on page 114 and fill in the chart on page 117.

More to Do
The children in Mrs. Woodard's class speak sign language. If you could speak another language, what would it be? Write 2 reasons why you would choose that language.

My Self-Check
I wrote the name of the language I would choose to learn. . . . .❏
I wrote 2 reasons why I would choose to learn it. . . . .❏

Understanding a Story Pattern

Knowing the pattern of a story helps you to read the story more easily and to know what might happen next.

1. Read "A Perfect Day?" and think about the pattern of the story as you're reading.
2. In the first box below, make a picture of everything or write words that tell what was happening in the story up to the word "Suddenly."
3. In the second box, make a picture of everything or write words that tell what was happening in the story after the word "Suddenly."

How Did I Do?

Check your answers with those on page 114 and fill in the chart on page 117.

A Perfect Day?

It was a beautiful day.

The sun was shining brightly.

The sun was shining brightly and the puffy white clouds were drifting through the blue sky.

The sun was shining brightly, the puffy white clouds were drifting through the blue sky, and the gentle breeze was carrying the chirping birds from tree to tree.

The sun was shining brightly, the puffy white clouds were drifting through the blue sky, the gentle breeze was carrying the chirping birds from tree to tree, and the flowers were dancing in the gardens.

The sun was shining brightly, the puffy white clouds were drifting through the blue sky, the gentle breeze was carrying the chirping birds from tree to tree, the flowers were dancing in the gardens, and the children were playing happily in the playground.

Suddenly, the puffy white clouds turned grey. The sky darkened as the sun quickly hid behind the clouds. The children stopped playing and looked up. The flowers stopped dancing and closed their petals. The birds sat still on the tree branches and hid their tiny faces under their wings. The gentle breeze became a wind.

A storm was on its way.

Choosing the Best Sentence Endings

Choosing the best endings for sentences from a story helps you to remember the details.

1. Reread "Silent Lotus."

2. Read the beginning of each sentence below and all the possible endings.

3. Choose the best ending. Check your thinking by looking in the story.

4. Put a circle around the letter that goes with the best answer.

Example:

Lotus and her mother and father lived

a) in Canada   b) on the edge of a lake   c) in a temple

1. Lotus

a) had a face as round as the moon   b) talked a lot   c) was always sad

2. Her mother and father named her Lotus because

a) she had eyes as bright as the stars   b) she was their only child

c) she made them think of the blossoms that covered the lake

3. Lotus

a) could not see   b) could not dance   c) could not hear or learn to speak

4. The first word that Lotus learned to say with her hands was

a) mother   b) lake   c) blossom

5. Most of all, Lotus liked to

a) go fishing with her father   b) weave baskets out of tall grasses

c) walk with the graceful birds

6. Inside the palace, Lotus and her mother and father saw

a) two lines of dancers   b) the queen and king   c) drums and cymbals

7. The king said

a) "She will learn to dance."   b) "She is a most beautiful child."

c) "Our daughter does not speak or hear."

8. The graceful old woman guided Lotus

a) happily   b) gracefully   c) patiently

9. As Lotus danced for all the people at the palace she saw

a) the beautiful silks   b) the pleasure and delight in the eyes of the people

c) the gold, jasmine flowers, precious stones, and pearls

10. Lotus became

a) a famous dancer in the Khmer kingdom   b) a dancing teacher

c) the most famous dancer in the Khmer kingdom

How Did I Do?

Check your answers with those on page 115 and fill in the chart on page 117.

Using Illustrations

Illustrations tell you a lot about a story. They can tell you about the characters, the setting, and what's happening in the story. Looking carefully at the illustrations can help you to "picture" the author's ideas.

1. Look at the illustrations in "Dava's Talent."

2. Circle the letter that best tells what is happening in each illustration.

Example: Which sentence tells what's happening in the illustration on page 45?

    a) Dava's papa was a shepherd.

    b) Dava loved the sheeps' cries and their thick coats.

    c) When Dava wanted the sheep to drink, they stood in the brook and splashed while Dava got wet and sneezy.

    d) Dava loved to play with the lambs.

1. Look at the illustration on page 45.

    a) Dava loved sheep.

    b) Dava's family lived near a river and mountains in a small village in Morocco.

    c) Dava couldn't herd the sheep very well.

    d) Dava loved the sheeps' cries and their thick coats.

2. Look at the illustration on page 46.

    a) Dava put on Papa's djellabah.

    b) The sheep thought Dava was a tree so they chewed on his sash.

    c) The sheep got into the garden and ate the melons.

    d) The sleeves of the djellabah covered his hands, and the hem dragged on the ground.

3. Look at the illustration on page 47.

    a) Dava began to sing in a loud voice.

    b) Leah chased Dava away from the house.

    c) Dava played the flute.

    d) "Your music sounds like rocks falling!" Leah said.

4. Look at the illustration across pages 48 and 49. Choose the **2** sentences that tell what's happening.

    a) Still whistling, Dava led the sheep toward the sheepcote.

    b) The frightened sheep moved toward the broken wall.

    c) Papa and Uncle Eban repaired the stone wall.

    d) Dava stood in the centre of the herd and whistled.

    e) The sheep were calm and Dava was calm.

How Did I Do?

Check your answers with those on page 115 and fill in the chart on page 117.

Finding Specific Information

When you read non-fiction, you need to read very carefully to help you find specific information. This helps you to be sure that you remember facts correctly.

1. Reread "Sounds Like Fun."
2. Read each sentence below.
3. Choose the best answer and print it on the line.

Example: The sound a dog makes. __bark__

1. What we hear when moving waves of air enter our ears. _____

2. These cause sounds. _____

3. These kinds of vocal cords produce sound waves. _____

4. Air is made up of this. _____

5. You can't see air because it is_____.

6. The ear sends sound waves through a series of tissues, liquids, and

   _____.

7. Messages are sent from the ear to here. _____

8. Hunters use them to help them find prey because they can hear high-pitched sounds.

   _____

9. What sound waves move through. _____

10. The brain translates this into sound. _____

dogs	molecules	vibrations
vibrating	bones	bark
brain	sound	air
movement	invisible	

How Did I Do?
Check your answers with those on page 115 and fill in the chart on page 117.

Checking Information

You may need to read a story more than once to be sure that you're thinking of the correct information.

1. Reread "Crabs for Dinner" to check for information.
2. Decide what is wrong with the information in each sentence.
3. Draw a line through the word that is wrong and write the correct word on the line.

Example: A smock is ~~food~~. __clothing__

1. Ghana is a place in Canada. _____

2. The family said grace after dinner. _____

3. A month before leaving for Ghana, Grandma invited the aunts and uncles for dinner.
   _____

4. The smock had circles of bright colors woven into it. _____

5. When Grandma was young, her mother told her lots of stories. _____

6. Uncle Robert rolled her eyes downward. _____

7. I ate a half bowl of fufu, soup, and a large piece of crab. _____

8. Grandma never ended her stories in a funny way. _____

9. Grandma's soup was spicy, cool, thick, and smooth. _____

10. Emily and I were eating hamburgers and the grown-ups were eating slime.

    _____

How Did I Do?
Check your answers with those on page 115 and fill in the chart on page 117.

More to Do
If you could have anything you wanted to eat for dinner today, what would be on your menu? Make a numbered list of the 5 foods you'd choose.

My Self-Check
I made a list. . . . .❑
I numbered my list from 1 to 5. . . . . . .❑

To accompany "Crabs for Dinner"

Following a Recipe

When you are following a recipe, you need to
- ➤ read all the directions first so you know what you're doing
- ➤ know what all the words mean
- ➤ follow the directions in order
- ➤ do exactly what the directions tell you

1. Read the "Mini Pizzas" recipe.

2. Answer the questions below.

Example: What word tells how to brush on the vegetable oil? <u>lightly</u>

1. What word means "what you need" to make this recipe? _____

2. What word means "what to do"? _____

3. What 3 ingredients can you add to make the pizzas even better?_____

_____, _____, and _____

4. What is the last thing the directions tell you to do? _____

5. How many steps should be done by an adult? _____

6. What kind of cheese slices should you use? _____

7. What word tells you the pizzas will be smaller than regular size? _____

8. What word tells you that you don't use whole mushrooms? _____

How Did I Do?

Check your answers with those on page 115 and fill in the chart on page 117.

More to Do

Write the name of your favourite food. Make a list of all the ingredients you can think of that are in it.

My Self-Check

I wrote the name of my favourite food. . . . .❏

I made a list of the ingredients. . . . .❏

To accompany "'Round the World Recipes"

Mini Pizzas

Follow this recipe to make mini pizzas. You will need an adult to do some of the steps. These steps are marked *.

Ingredients

English muffins

Vegetable oil

Small jar of pizza sauce

Mozzarella cheese slices

Sliced mushrooms

Pepperoni

Chopped onion

Directions

1. *Cut each muffin in half.

2. Brush vegetable oil lightly onto the top of each muffin.

3. Cover each half of the muffin with pizza sauce.

4. Put 1/2 slice cheese on each.

5. Add extra toppings of sliced mushrooms, pepperoni, and chopped onion if you like.

6. *Microwave on high until cheese melts—about 1 minute for each pizza—or bake in a regular oven for 15–20 minutes at 160°C.

7. *Remove from oven.

8. Let the pizzas cool.

9. Eat and enjoy!

Classifying Details

You can classify details by grouping related details together. To do this, decide on the main ideas, then find details that give more information about each of the ideas.

1. Read "Creating Fog in a Bottle."
2. Read each idea below. Write **N** if it tells something about What You **N**eed, **D** if it tells something about What to **D**o, or **L** if it tells something about What to **L**ook For.

Example:
__N__ a surface such as a desk, a table, or a counter

_____ put a strainer over the mouth of the jar

_____ hot tap water

_____ fog will start to form on the inside of the jar

_____ a strainer

_____ pour out all the water except for 25 mm

_____ several ice cubes

_____ fill the strainer with ice cubes

_____ a large jar or a wide-mouthed bottle

_____ watch for a while

_____ fill the jar with hot water

How Did I Do?
Check your answers with those on page 116 and fill in the chart on page 117.

More to Do
Fold a piece of paper into 3 sections.
In section 1, sketch the 5 things you need to make fog in a bottle. Label your sketches.
In section 2, make sketches to show what to do.
In section 3, make a sketch to show what should happen.

My Self-Check
I folded my paper into 3 sections. . . . . ❑
In section 1, I sketched and labelled 5 things I would need. . . . . ❑
In section 2, I made sketches to show what to do. . . . . ❑
In section 3, I made a sketch of what to look for. ❑

To accompany "Touch It, Taste It"

Creating Fog in a Bottle

To make fog in a bottle, you need a large jar or a wide-mouthed bottle, hot tap water, a strainer, several ice cubes, and a surface such as a table, a desk, or a counter to put the jar on. Start your experiment by filling the jar with hot water. Carefully pour out all of the hot water except for 25 mm. Put a strainer over the mouth of the jar and fill the strainer with ice cubes. Watch for a while, and before too long the cold air from the ice cubes will meet the hot air from the water. When this happens, fog will start to form on the inside of the jar.

To accompany "Touch It, Taste It"

Understanding Similes

Similes can help you to understand what you're reading because they help you to make pictures in your mind. Similes usually begin with "like" or "as."

1. Read the simile sentences and underline the simile in each sentence.
2. In the chart, record the 2 things that are being compared.
3. Record the word that tells what they have in common.

Example: <u>Mary ran as fast as a gazelle</u> to win the race.

What's Being Compared		What They Have in Common
Mary	gazelle	fast
1.		
2.		
3.		
4.		
5.		
6.		
7.		
8.		
9.		
10.		

How Did I Do?

Check your answers with those on page 116 and fill in the chart on page 117.

More to Do

Fold a sheet of paper into 4 sections. Choose your 4 favourite similes from the simile sentences. In each section of the paper, draw your own picture to show what the simile means.

My Self-Check

I folded the paper into 4 sections. .... ❑
I chose my 4 favourite similes. .... ❑
My pictures show what the similes mean. .... ❑

To accompany "Chimes and Tingles"

Simile Sentences

1. Anna's hands were as cold as ice when she came in from outside.

2. The jumbo jet soared like an eagle up into the sky.

3. My new jacket felt as comfortable as an old shoe.

4. The Canadian prairies are as flat as a pancake.

5. The candy was as hard as a rock.

6. Rashif was as hungry as a bear when he got home for dinner.

7. Marissa sat like a bump on a log because she didn't want to play.

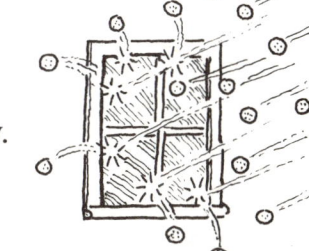

8. My teacher is as wise as an owl.

9. The hail was as loud as golf balls being thrown against a window.

10. The cake crumbled in my hand like pieces of broken stone.

To accompany "Chimes and Tingles"

Finding Information

Sometimes you may need to reread parts of an article to be sure that you remember the facts correctly. To do this, skim the information to look for headings and key words that will help you find the right part. Then read carefully to find the information.

1. Reread "What a Feeling!" to find the creatures described in the following sentences.
2. When you find the answer, write the creature's name on the line.
   Hint: Some creatures will be used more than once.

Example: Has the most poisonous tentacles and barbs. <u>lion's mane jellyfish</u>

1. Is a Canadian nightjar with bristles. _____

2. Has barbels that can be tucked away under its chin. _____

3. Eats crab, mollusks, sea urchins, squid, and fish. _____ and

   _____

4. Has one pair of long, ribbonlike barbels. _____

5. Has tentacles that hang in the water. _____

6. Its barbels stick out from its nose, jaw, and chin. _____

7. Has whiskers that can feel along the ocean bottom for food.

   _____ and _____

8. Is the only mammal that doesn't use whiskers to feel with. _____

9. Can find and scoop up insects as it flies through the air. _____

10. Is a nocturnal species of nightjar that lives in Australia. _____

11. Has feathers called semi-bristles. _____

12. Eats fish, shrimp, and crab. _____

13. Has eight barbels. _____

How Did I Do?
Check your answers with those on page 116 and fill in the chart on page 117.

Identifying Characters, Setting, and Storyline

When you finish reading a story, you know where and when the story took place (setting), you've met the characters, and you know what the story was about (storyline, plot).

1. Reread "Pettranella."

2. Read the following sentence starters and circle the answer that completes the sentence.

Example: One of the characters in "Pettranella" was
      a) a doctor   b) a shopkeeper   c) a neighbour

1. The most important character in the story is
    a) Grandmother   b) Mother   c) Pettranella

2. The main setting (when and where the story happens) is
    a) long ago in a country far away   b) one summer in Canada
    c) long ago in Manitoba

3. This story is mostly about
    a) how a family settled in a new country   b) planting a vegetable garden
    c) fixing a broken ox cart

4. When the day came for Pettranella to leave her homeland, she was
    a) sick   b) sad and excited   c) excited

5. The family travelled to the new country in
    a) a jumbo jet   b) a train   c) a big boat

6. The first sign of spring that Pettranella saw was
    a) flowers blooming   b) a black ox   c) geese flying north

7. The family travelled to their homestead by
    a) horse and buggy   b) ox cart   c) covered wagon

8. Pettranella knew where she'd lost the seeds when
    a) she reached into her pocket and pulled them out   b) spring came
    c) the neighbours came to visit

9. Pettranella's new home was
    a) a tall, narrow house   b) a small cabin
    c) a bed of spruce and tamarack boughs

10. The story ended
    a) happily, because Pettranella made lots of friends
    b) sadly, because the neighbors didn't come to visit very often
    c) happily, because Pettranella was able to keep her promise to her grandmother

How Did I Do?

Check your answers with those on page 118 and fill in the chart on page 121.

Using a Timeline

Timelines organize information. A timeline tells you
➤ what happened
➤ when the event happened
➤ the order in which the events happened

1. Read the questions below.
2. Read the timeline to find the answers.
3. Circle the letter of the correct answer or write the answer on the line.

Examples: When was television invented?
      a) 1896   (b) 1923
      c) 1964   d) early in the 1800s

      It's been used since 1800 to take photographs. <u>camera</u>

1. What was invented in 1908?
    a) the electric guitar   b) Velcro
    c) refrigerator   d) zipper

2. Which of the following was invented first?
    a) sliced bread   b) Frisbee
    c) vacuum cleaner   d) snowmobile

3. Which of the following is the newest invention?
    a) television   b) refrigerator
    c) electric guitar   d) clothes dryer

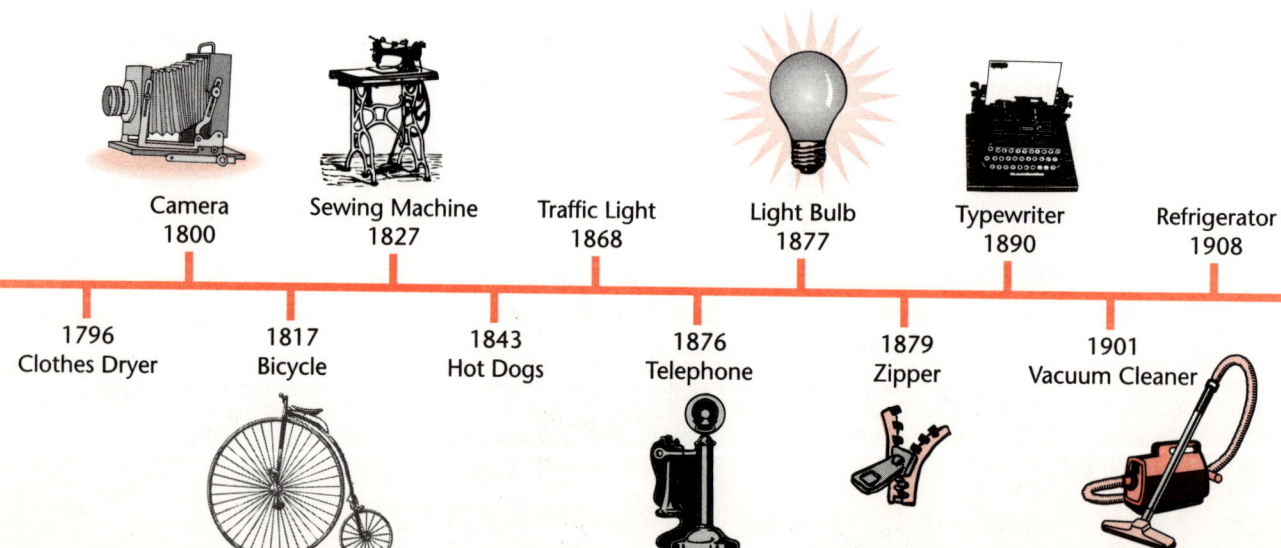

Camera 1800   Sewing Machine 1827   Traffic Light 1868   Light Bulb 1877   Typewriter 1890   Refrigerator 1908

1796 Clothes Dryer   1817 Bicycle   1843 Hot Dogs   1876 Telephone   1879 Zipper   1901 Vacuum Cleaner

To accompany "A Pioneer Child's Day"

4. Which invention was created since you were born?
   a) Post-it Notes   b) DVDs
   c) compact disks   d) Velcro

5. When were people first able to talk voice-to-voice with other people? _____

6. What invention from 1929 can replace zippers or laces? _____

7. Since 1901, the _____ has helped to keep things clean.

8. Before the invention of the _____ in 1908, it was hard to keep food cold.

9. After this invention in 1927, people didn't have to use a knife to cut a loaf into sections. _____

10. A musical instrument that you plug in was invented in what year? _____

How Did I Do?

Check your answers with those on page 118 and fill in the chart on page 121.

More to Do

Choose the invention from the list in the timeline that you think is the most important. Draw a picture of the invention you've selected. Print the name of the invention below the picture. Write a sentence to tell why you think the invention is important.

My Self-Check

I drew a picture of the invention. . . . . ☐
I printed the name of the invention below the picture. . . . . ☐
I wrote one sentence to tell why it's an important invention. . . . . ☐

Television 1923   Velcro 1929   Frisbee 1945   Computer Mouse 1959   Compact Disc (CD) 1973   Digital Video Disc (DVD) 1995

1921 Electric Guitar   1927 Sliced Bread   1943 Computer   1948 Snowmobile   1964 The Internet   1980 Post-it Notes Space Shuttle

Finding Information in Illustrations

Looking at illustrations is like reading words. The more carefully you look and think about illustrations, the more information you can get from them.

1. Reread "More Than Anything Else" and look carefully at the illustrations.
2. Answer the questions below.

Example:
In the illustration on the cover of *Carving New Frontiers*,
a) how many people are in the car? _4_
b) are the women in the front seat or the back seat? _back seat_

1. In the illustration on page 20,
a) what is Papa carrying in his left hand? _____
b) what are all 3 people wearing on their heads? _____

2. In the illustration on page 21,
a) what are the people shovelling? _____ b) what do they put the salt into? _____

3. In the illustration on page 22,
a) what are the people sitting on? _____
b) what are they wearing on their feet? _____

4. In the illustration on page 23,
a) what is giving light? _____
b) how many people have gathered together to listen? _____

5. In the illustration on page 24,
a) how many people are in the boy's family? _____
b) who is the boy speaking to? _____

6. In the illustration at the top of page 25,
a) what is Mama giving to the boy? _____ b) how is Mama feeling? _____

7. In the illustration at the bottom of page 25,
a) what is giving light? _____ b) what is the boy printing? _____

8. In the illustration on page 26,
a) on which foot is the boy standing? _____
b) where is the lantern? _____ c) how is the boy feeling? _____

9. In the illustration on page 27,
a) what is the man printing? _____ b) is the man right- or
left-handed? _____ c) where is the man printing? _____

How Did I Do?

Check your answers with those on page 118 and fill in the chart on page 121.

Finding Words That Go Together

Words can be grouped together for many reasons. Some words go together because they rhyme. Some words are grouped because their meanings go together—one thing holds the other.

1. Reread "General Store" and write the words from the poem that rhyme with each of the words below.

Example: sun – <u>fun</u>

   1. lunches – _____

   2. wide – _____

   3. say – _____

   4. string – _____

   5. shelf – _____

   6. bright – _____

   7. door – _____

2. Write the words from the poem that tell what container holds each of the things below.

Example: flour comes in <u>sacks</u>

   8. bananas come in _____

   9. sugar comes in _____

  10. peppermint comes in _____

  11. string comes in _____

  12. seeds come in _____

  13. tea comes in _____

  14. calico comes in _____

  15. rubber boots come in _____

How Did I Do?

Check your answers with those on page 118 and fill in the chart on page 121.

More to Do

Imagine you own a store. Write 3 sentences to tell about it. In sentence 1, tell what kind of store it would be. In sentence 2, tell what you would sell. In sentence 3, tell what you would name your store.

My Self-Check

I wrote 3 sentences. . . . . ❑

My first sentence tells the kind of store I would own. . . . . . . ❑

My second sentence tells what I would sell. . . . . ❑

My last sentence tells the name of the store. . . . . ❑

Making Good Guesses

Sometimes the answer to a question isn't stated right in the story. So, you have to think about what the story does tell you and make a good guess.

1. Reread "How Two-Feather Was Saved from Loneliness."
2. Read the sentence starters in Column A. Then read the endings in Column B.
3. Draw a line from each sentence starter to the best ending.

Column A   **Column B**

Example:
Two-Feather held the ears of corn ———— to remind him of the figure.

Two-Feather was lonely because   the sun.

Two-Feather slept a lot because   he wanted to forget how lonely he was.

Two-Feather had never seen fire because   there was no one around.

Instead of fire, Two-Feather used   his hands.

To dig out the roots from under the   no one knew how to make it.
snow, Two-Feather used

4. Answer the following questions in a sentence.

What did Two-Feather use for

a) a mirror? _____

b) a bed? _____

c) transportation? _____

d) matches? _____

e) a grocery store? _____

How Did I Do?

Check your answers with those on page 119 and fill in the chart on page 121.

To accompany "How Two-Feather Was Saved from Loneliness"

Finding Specific Information

When you read non-fiction, you need to read very carefully to help find specific information. This helps you to be sure that you remember facts correctly.

1. Reread "Fire Dragons and Flying Money."
2. Read each question below.
3. Write your answer to complete the sentence.

Example:

Scientists have made a lot of what?

Scientists have made a lot of <u>inventions and discoveries.</u>

1. Where were many important discoveries first made?
   Many important discoveries were first made _____

2. When was paper first made?
   Paper was first made _____

3. Why were the paper sheets that were peeled off the screens hung up?
   The paper sheets were hung up _____

4. How would a lodestone always turn?
   A lodestone _____

5. What did fishers use to carry their fishing lines?
   Fishers used _____

6. What did the Chinese use lodestone to tell them?
   The Chinese used lodestone to _____

7. Who is the author of "Fire Dragons and Flying Money"?
   The author is _____

8. When did the Chinese invent a special kind of china called "porcelain"?
   The Chinese invented porcelain _____

9. Where were the cocoons of silkworms soaked?
   The cocoons of silkworms were soaked _____

10. When the Chinese made paper, what was left behind on the screen?
    When the Chinese made paper, _____

How Did I Do?

Check your answers with those on page 119 and fill in the chart on page 121.

Recognizing Text Formats

Authors present information in different ways. Sometimes authors arrange information in paragraphs, as a list, or as questions and answers.

1. Read "Up, Up, and Away!" and look at how the information is organized.
2. Read the questions below.
3. Circle the letter of the best answer or write the answer on the line.

Example:
What short form is used for "Question"?
a) Q and A   b) Answer   c) Q   d) A

1. Which of the following describes how the information in "Up, Up, and Away!" is organized?
   a) poetry   b) paragraphs   c) list   d) questions and answers

2. What 3 clues help you to find the questions quickly? (circle 3 answers)
   a) the questions are usually longer than the answers
   b) the questions are printed in bold.
   c) the questions end with a question mark
   d) the questions are usually shorter than the answers

3. What short form is used for "Answer"?
   a) Q   b) A   c) Q and A   d) Question

4. Questions often begin with **how**, **why**, **when**, **where**, **what**, or **who**. In "Up, Up, and Away!" which of these question words is not used?
   a) what   b) why   c) when   d) where   e) who   f) how

5. "Who" questions are answered by naming a person or persons. Name the persons who invented the airplane. _____

6. "When" questions are answered by telling a time. Tell when an airplane can get up off the ground. _____

7. "What" questions are answered by naming a thing. Tell what an airplane that flaps its wings is called. _____

8. "Why" questions are answered by giving a reason. Tell why an airplane can get up into the air. _____

How Did I Do?

Check your answers with those on page 119 and fill in the chart on page 121.

To accompany "The Inventor Thinks Up Helicopters"

Up, Up, and Away!

Q: What kinds of airplanes flap their wings like birds do to get up into the air?

A: Some small, light airplanes flap their wings to get up into the air.

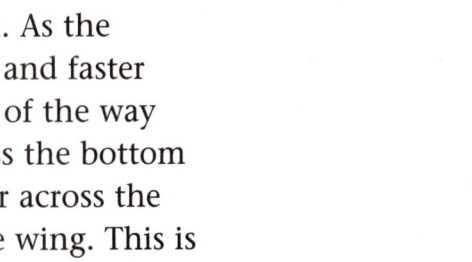

Q: What are these airplanes called?

A: They're called "ornithopters."

Q: Why don't all airplanes flap their wings?

A: Airplanes that carry people don't flap their wings because they're too heavy.

Q: Why is an airplane able to get up into the air?

A: The reason that airplanes can get up into the air is because of air pressure.

Q: How is air pressure created?

A: When the airplane starts moving down the runway, air hits the wings and moves across the top and bottom of them. As the airplane moves faster and faster, the air moves faster and faster across the top and bottom of the wings. But because of the way the airplane's wings are curved, more air passes across the bottom of the wing than the top. This makes the air go faster across the top of the wing than it goes across the bottom of the wing. This is called "air pressure."

Q: When can the airplane leave the ground?

A: When there is enough air pressure on the bottom of the wing, it begins to push upward and starts to lift the airplane into the air.

Q: What is the name for this push?

A: This push is called "lift." As this lift becomes larger and larger, and therefore stronger and stronger, the airplane goes higher and higher into the air.

Q: Who invented the airplane?

A: The Wright Brothers (Orville and Wilbur) are the inventors of the airplane.

To accompany "The Inventor Thinks Up Helicopters"

Checking Details

You can reread a story to check details you may not have noticed or remembered the first time. This helps you to understand what you have read.

1. Reread "The Very Clever Device" to check for details.

2. Decide what information is wrong in each sentence.

3. Draw a line through the word or words that are wrong and write the correct word(s) on the line.

Example: Mary was proud of having a job and earning ~~a lot.~~ __something__ .

1. For years, answering the ringing bells in her best speaking voice had been fun.

_____

2. It was her friend Iris, who was the switchboard girl in the next city. _____

3. Her father and brothers had been talking about automobiles for the last few

days, so she knew what they were. _____

4. By afternoon everyone who could walk lined the streets. _____

5. The whole town was watching the twisty, red brick road when the automobile

appeared as a tiny black bump on the horizon. _____

6. Mary was a little bored as she walked down the wooden sidewalk to

her house. _____

7. Mary opened her O. Hinty mystery story and started to read. _____

8. "But I wouldn't want to own one," her brother Travis said earlier at dinner.

_____

9. Papa disagreed. "It took a lot of doing to think of such a thing, and then

actually make it." _____

10. Mama said, "I don't think an automobile will ever be seen around here again."

_____

How Did I Do?

Check your answers with those on page 120 and fill in the chart on page 121.

Knowing Fact from Fiction

A "fact" is something that is known to be true or real. "Fiction" is something that is made up or imagined.

1. Read the sentences and think about whether you think each statement is fact or fiction.

2. Read "Pluto Facts" to find out. Underline the proof in the text.

3. Write **fact** or **fiction** on the line following each sentence.

Example: A lot is known about Pluto. <u>fiction</u>

1. Pluto is covered in sand. _____

2. Pluto has many moons. _____

3. Because Pluto is so far from the Sun, it's always in darkness. _____

4. Pluto is a medium-sized planet. _____

5. A spacecraft has never gone to Pluto. _____

Pluto Facts

There are 9 planets in our solar system. They are Mercury, Jupiter, Saturn, Uranus, Mars, Earth, Venus, Neptune, and Pluto. We live on the planet Earth. For a long time, we thought there were only 8 planets. Then Pluto was discovered. Here are some interesting "Pluto Facts."

- <u>Not much is known about Pluto.</u>
- If you use the most powerful telescope to look at Pluto, you'll only be able to see the largest features on its surface.
- Pluto seems to be lying on its "side."
- Although Pluto can be seen with a low power telescope, you need many months of careful looking just to find it in the sky.
- Pluto is a rocky planet.
- Pluto has one moon, called "Charon."
- Scientists are still uncertain what it's made of.
- Pluto is the only planet that has not been visited by a spacecraft.
- Photographs of Pluto are very blurry because it's so far away.
- Pluto is so far from the Sun that it is always in darkness.
- Pluto is the smallest of the 9 planets.

Maybe someday we will learn more about this mysterious, far-away planet.

How Did I Do?

Check your answers with those on page 120 and fill in the chart on page 121.

Finding Missing Information

You may need to reread non-fiction to help you find important details. This helps you to be sure that you remember the information correctly.

1. Reread "Hawaii, Here We Come!" to find the missing information.
2. Write the information on the line.

Example: Sam and his <u>family</u> went to Hawaii.

1. Sam's diary begins on _____ 24 and ends on June _____ .

2. On May 24, Sam wrote about his last day at _____ with his _____ .

3. May 25: Sam wrote about how sick everyone was feeling, except for his _____ .

4. On May 27, all Sam was able to write was "_____ today."

5. May 29: Sam writes that all the sails have been _____ .

6. On June 6, Sam wrote that Charlie had found a _____ , Sam couldn't see for almost a _____ , and that Charlie and Sam had been reading about _____ .

7. June 7: Sam thinks they get to Hawaii in about a _____ .

8. On June 12, Sam writes that it was too cold a week before and that it's almost too _____ now!

9. On June 14, Sam is so excited. He writes: "I CAN'T _____ !!!"

10. June 15, Sam wrote that after exactly _____ weeks at sea, he's not sure if he'll even be able to _____ properly on land again.

How Did I Do?

Check your answers with those on page 120 and fill in the chart on page 121.

More to Do

If you could go anywhere in the world, where would it be?
Write where you would go, how you would travel there, and why you would like to go there.

My Self-Check

I wrote the name of the place I would choose. . . . . . . ❏
I told how I would travel there. . . . . ❏
I gave a reason why I would like to go there. . . . . . . ❏

To accompany "Hawaii, Here We Come!"

Matching Words and Meanings

When you read a story, you may meet words you don't know. You can
- ➤ reread the sentence the word is in to get more information
- ➤ decide on a meaning that makes sense
- ➤ use a dictionary to check if you have the right meaning

1. Reread "Marisol and the Yellow Messenger" to find the word that answers each riddle below.
2. Write the word on the line.

Example: This Spanish word means "ocean" and "sun." <u>Marisol</u>

1. What Marisol did with her cold feet by dragging them along the ground. _____

2. This place is Spain for Marisol because she was born there. _____

3. What the wooden spoon was used for so the bird could rest at night. _____

4. What the bird's wings did by flapping quickly and softly. _____

5. A swinging bed where Marisol used to rock with her grandpa. _____

perch	homeland	fluttered
shuffled	hammock	Marisol

How Did I Do?
Check your answers with those on page 120 and fill in the chart on page 121.

More to Do
Fold a sheet of paper into 2 sections. Read each riddle and draw a picture of the answer.
- a building where teachers go to teach and children go to learn
- a water animal that has gills, fins, and scales

Print a word label on each picture to answer the riddle.

My Self-Check
I drew 2 pictures to answer the riddles. . . . . ❑
I labelled each picture. . . . . ❑

Identifying Authors and Illustrators

Authors write words to give messages. Illustrators make pictures to give messages. Knowing about the authors and illustrators helps you to understand what they are saying.

1. Reread "My Wish for Tomorrow."
2. Read the questions below.
3. Circle the letter that goes with the correct answer or write the answer on the line.

Example:
Which author wrote about wanting everyone to share the world with the animals and trees?
a) Nadezsha   b) Ynthis   c) Kristel   d) Renato

1. Which author wrote about flying around the world to make friends?
   a) Samantha   b) Nery   c) Tasha   d) Sonali

2. Which author wrote about nobody being left out in games?
   a) Cheryl   b) Agnieszka   c) Rachel   d) Tasha

3. Which author wrote about wishing that everyone would love each other for what they are?
   a) Sonali   b) Agnieszka   c) Akanksha   d) Eduardo

4. Which author wrote about wanting people to stop fighting and be friends?
   a) Samantha   b) Meadhbh   c) Cynthia   d) Tasha

5. What is the first name of the illustrator who made a picture of

   a) a heart with wings? _____

   b) flowers, grass, a butterfly, the sun, mountains, and a blue sky? _____

   c) a sun? _____

   d) lots of people, ladders, balloons, birds, and more? _____

   e) a girl standing beside a house? _____

6. Where do these children live?

   a) Vicky _____   b) Renato _____   c) Samantha _____

7. How old are these children?

   a) Samantha _____   b) Fortunate _____   c) Peta _____

How Did I Do?
Check your answers with those on page 120 and fill in the chart on page 121.

To accompany "My Wish for Tomorrow"

How to Self-Check Your Work

The answers for each page start here.
Your teacher may want you to pull out the answer section and file it. You can then find each answer page as you need it and set it beside the page you are marking.

Title of the page you did.

Number of marks you give for the correct answers

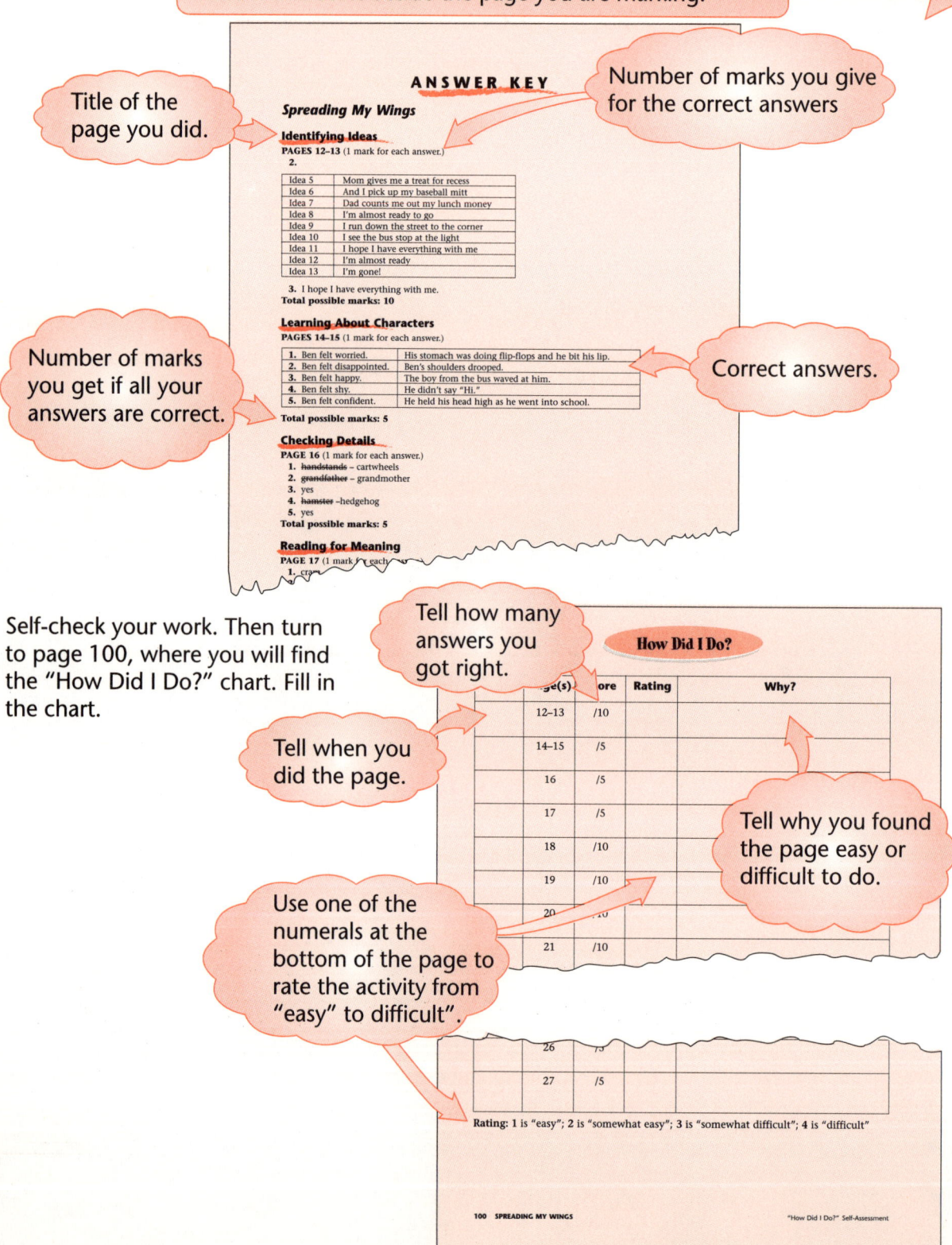

ANSWER KEY

Spreading My Wings

Identifying Ideas
PAGES 12–13 (1 mark for each answer.)
2.

Idea 5	Mom gives me a treat for recess
Idea 6	And I pick up my baseball mitt
Idea 7	Dad counts me out my lunch money
Idea 8	I'm almost ready to go
Idea 9	I run down the street to the corner
Idea 10	I see the bus stop at the light
Idea 11	I hope I have everything with me
Idea 12	I'm almost ready
Idea 13	I'm gone!

3. I hope I have everything with me.
Total possible marks: 10

Learning About Characters
PAGES 14–15 (1 mark for each answer.)

1. Ben felt worried.	His stomach was doing flip-flops and he bit his lip.
2. Ben felt disappointed.	Ben's shoulders drooped.
3. Ben felt happy.	The boy from the bus waved at him.
4. Ben felt shy.	He didn't say "Hi."
5. Ben felt confident.	He held his head high as he went into school.

Total possible marks: 5

Checking Details
PAGE 16 (1 mark for each answer.)
1. ~~handstands~~ – cartwheels
2. ~~grandfather~~ – grandmother
3. yes
4. ~~hamster~~ –hedgehog
5. yes
Total possible marks: 5

Reading for Meaning
PAGE 17 (1 mark for each...
1. cra...

Number of marks you get if all your answers are correct.

Correct answers.

Self-check your work. Then turn to page 100, where you will find the "How Did I Do?" chart. Fill in the chart.

Tell how many answers you got right.

Tell when you did the page.

Use one of the numerals at the bottom of the page to rate the activity from "easy" to difficult".

Tell why you found the page easy or difficult to do.

How Did I Do?

...ge(s)	...ore	Rating	Why?
12–13	/10		
14–15	/5		
16	/5		
17	/5		
18	/10		
19	/10		
20	/10		
21	/10		
26	/5		
27	/5		

Rating: 1 is "easy"; 2 is "somewhat easy"; 3 is "somewhat difficult"; 4 is "difficult"

100   SPREADING MY WINGS   "How Did I Do?" Self-Assessment

ANSWER KEY

Spreading My Wings

Identifying Ideas

PAGES 12–13 (1 mark for each answer.)

2.

Idea 5	Mom gives me a treat for recess
Idea 6	And I pick up my baseball mitt
Idea 7	Dad counts me out my lunch money
Idea 8	I'm almost ready to go
Idea 9	I run down the street to the corner
Idea 10	I see the bus stop at the light
Idea 11	I hope I have everything with me
Idea 12	I'm almost ready
Idea 13	I'm gone!

3. I hope I have everything with me.

Total possible marks: 10

Learning About Characters

PAGES 14–15 (1 mark for each answer.)

1. Ben felt worried.	His stomach was doing flip-flops and he bit his lip.
2. Ben felt disappointed.	Ben's shoulders drooped.
3. Ben felt happy.	The boy from the bus waved at him.
4. Ben felt shy.	He didn't say "Hi."
5. Ben felt confident.	He held his head high as he went into school.

Total possible marks: 5

Checking Details

PAGE 16 (1 mark for each answer.)

1. ~~handstands~~ – cartwheels
2. ~~grandfather~~ – grandmother
3. yes
4. ~~hamster~~ –hedgehog
5. yes

Total possible marks: 5

Reading for Meaning

PAGE 17 (1 mark for each answer.)

1. cram
2. tied
3. rush
4. noiselessly
5. softly

Total possible marks: 5

Understanding Characters

PAGE 18 (1 mark for each answer.)

1.	Valerie	6.	jealous
2.	Steven	7.	safe
3.	Trey	8.	lonely
4.	Juanita	9.	proud
5.	Maura	10.	worried

Total possible marks: 10

Following Story Events

PAGE 19 (1 mark for each answer.)

2.

6	Gita put the chimes in Mr. Flinch's mailbox.
2	Gita wandered outside to look at the hole she had dug.
7	Gita heard a soft tinkling sound.
10	Gita asked Mr. Flinch to help her plant the First Rose.
8	Mr. Flinch asked Gita to help him hang the chimes.
4	Mr. Flinch growled at Gita.
9	Mr. Flinch gave Gita a bouquet of roses.
5	Gita saw Mr. Flinch playing the violin.
3	Gita looked over the fence at her neighbour's garden.

3. Gita put the chimes in Mr. Flinch's mailbox.

Total possible marks: 10

Listing Facts to Compare

PAGE 20 (1 mark for each answer. Your answers may be worded a little differently.)

Shirley
– has blue sneakers
– has a bracelet
– has a blue beret
– has stripes down pants
– has hearts on her shirt
– has red hair
– has blue eyes
– has a V-neck shirt
– has pierced ears
– has a friend

Total possible marks: 10

Reading New Words

PAGE 21 (1 mark for each answer.)

1.	unpacking	6.	distance
2.	repeated	7.	famous
3.	cobwebs	8.	peppermint
4.	blanket	9.	actually
5.	scuffing	10.	regular

Total possible marks: 10

Following a Recipe

PAGE 22-23 (1 mark for each answer. Your answers may be worded a little differently.)
1. a large bowl and a small bowl
2. Turn on the oven.
3. 180°C
4. flour, sugar, baking soda, and baking powder
5. wooden spoon
6. I need to beat the egg.
7. 325 mL buttermilk
8. into the loaf pan
9. about 1 hour
10. It will be golden brown.

Total possible marks: 10

Finding the Cause

PAGE 24-25 (1 mark for each answer. Your answers may be worded a little differently.)
1. The horse's shoe was loose.
2. The horse's shoe came off.
3. The miller left his horse and cart to look for the horseshoe.
4. When the miller returned, the horse and cart were gone.
5. The miller lost everything.

Total possible marks: 5

Checking the Meaning

PAGE 26 (1 mark for each answer.)

Word	The Meaning I Chose
1. preserve	keep alive
2. transplanted	moved to another place
3. patience	ability to wait calmly
4. challenged	invited to participate
5. invading	infesting (or taking over)

Total possible marks: 5

Checking Information

PAGE 27 (1 mark for each answer.)
1. b) The cages were clean, the water was fresh, and the budgies were happy.
2. a) She was unhappy that the big catfish was in such a small space.
3. b) He thought the person who captured it was mistreating it.
4. b) The catfish tank was empty.
5. b) The store was called "The Catfish Palace."

Total possible marks: 5

How Did I Do?

Date	Page(s)	Score	Rating	Why?
	12–13	/10		
	14–15	/5		
	16	/5		
	17	/5		
	18	/10		
	19	/10		
	20	/10		
	21	/10		
	22–23	/10		
	24–25	/5		
	26	/5		
	27	/5		

Rating: 1 is "easy"; **2** is "somewhat easy"; **3** is "somewhat difficult"; **4** is "difficult"

Tales—Princesses, Peas, and Enchanted Trees

Understanding Characters

PAGE 28 (1 mark for each answer. Your order may not be the same, and some of your answers may be worded a little differently.)

Character(s)	Description	Experience
1. Elves	mischievous, generous, small	Title: <u>The Shoemaker and the Elves</u> In return for new suits they left good luck behind.
2. Iktomi	vain, foolish, greedy	Title: <u>Iktomi and the Berries</u> Because of his greed his clothes were ruined.
3. Maru-Me	strong, funny, mischievous	Title: <u>Three Strong Women</u> She proved she had much to teach a strong man.
4. Vasilisa	beautiful, brave	Title: <u>Baba Yaga and Vasilisa the Brave</u> She was helped by a doll.
5. Yi	mighty, fierce, brave	Title: <u>Too Many Suns</u> He gave the world warmth and light.

Total possible marks: 20

Reading for Meaning

PAGE 29 (1 mark for each answer.)
1. lovely
2. smelled
3. found
4. mad
5. entirely

Total possible marks: 5

Retelling a Story

PAGE 30 (1 mark for each answer that is in your own words and that has a meaning similar to the answer given here.)

Once a prince was looking for a real princess to marry. <u>He travelled all over the world</u> and met many princesses, but he was never sure that <u>they were true princesses.</u>

One evening <u>a terrible storm</u> raged around the palace. There was <u>thunder</u> and lightning and <u>rain came down in torrents.</u> Suddenly <u>a knocking was heard on the palace gate</u> and <u>the old king</u> went to open it.

Standing in front of the gate was a princess, but what a sight she was with <u>water running down from her hair and her clothes!</u> She announced <u>that she was a real princess.</u>

The old queen decided she would <u>find out if the princess was real.</u> So she went into the bedroom, <u>laid a pea</u> on the bottom of the mattress, piled <u>twenty mattresses on top</u>, and then put <u>twenty eiderdown beds on top of the mattresses.</u> The princess <u>had to lie on this all night.</u>

<u>In the morning</u>, when she was asked how she had slept, the princess answered, <u>"I have scarcely shut my eyes all night.</u> There must have been something hard in the bed because <u>I am black and blue all over my body."</u>

And so they knew she was a real princess, for <u>only real princesses could be as sensitive as that.</u> The prince <u>married this real princess</u>, and the pea was placed <u>in the Art Museum.</u>

Total possible marks: 20

Sorting Text from a Play

PAGE 31 (1 mark for each answer.)

1. *At left are woods, represented by old tree.* | Setting |
2. *MS. MOUSE sits in rocking chair, sewing.* | Setting |
3. UNCLE RAT: Where will the wedding supper be? | Character lines |
4. *(They point left.)* | Character direction |
5. *Meadow, near hollow tree.* | Setting |
6. *MOTH enters, carrying tablecloth.* | Setting |
7. BUG: Three green beans and a black-eyed pea. | Character lines |
8. *(Remains standing to announce other visitors)* | Character direction |
9. CHICK: I ate so much it made me sick. | Character lines |
10. *(All sing "Mr. Frog Went A-Courtin'.")* | Character direction |

Total possible marks: 10

Finding Information

PAGE 32-33 (1 mark for each answer.)

1. Mom was baking a birthday cake.	G
2. First Kwan volunteered to go on the errand.	S
3. Grandma liked to read the Saturday newspaper.	G
4. Mom needed flour, candles, and a newspaper.	S
5. Loc thought he could remember better than anyone else.	S
6. Nikki took more time to go to the store than her brothers did.	G
7. Loc could only remember one item on the list.	S
8. Kwan and Loc thought Nikki would not be able to do the errand.	G
9. Nikki entered the store saying, "Flour, candles, newspaper."	S
10. Mom was proud of Nikki.	G

Total possible marks: 10

Reading New Words

PAGE 34 (1 mark for each answer.)

1. enchantment [en – chant – ment]
2. invisible [in – vis – i – ble]
3. mistreated [mis – treat – ed]
4. festival [fes – ti – val]
5. object [ob – ject]
6. kimono [ki – mo – no]
7. Algonquin [Al – gon – quin]
8. nobleman [no – ble – man]
9. adventures [ad – ven – tures]
10. delighted [de – light – ed]

Total possible marks: 20

Interpreting Poem Ideas

1. The tortoise was sure he could beat the hare.	Tortoise answered, "Slow as day, I'll outrun you anyway."
2. The two animals built a track in the shape of an egg.	An oval racetrack They laid out
3. After he ran part of the race, the hare went to sleep.	Then halfway there, Hare took a nap,
4. Tortoise passed Hare as he slept.	So tortoise caught him On that lap.
5. By taking a nap the hare lost the race.	Hare dreamed his winning Quite away,

Total possible marks: 5

Diagramming Story Plot

PAGES 36–37 (1 mark for each answer. Your answers may be worded a little differently.)

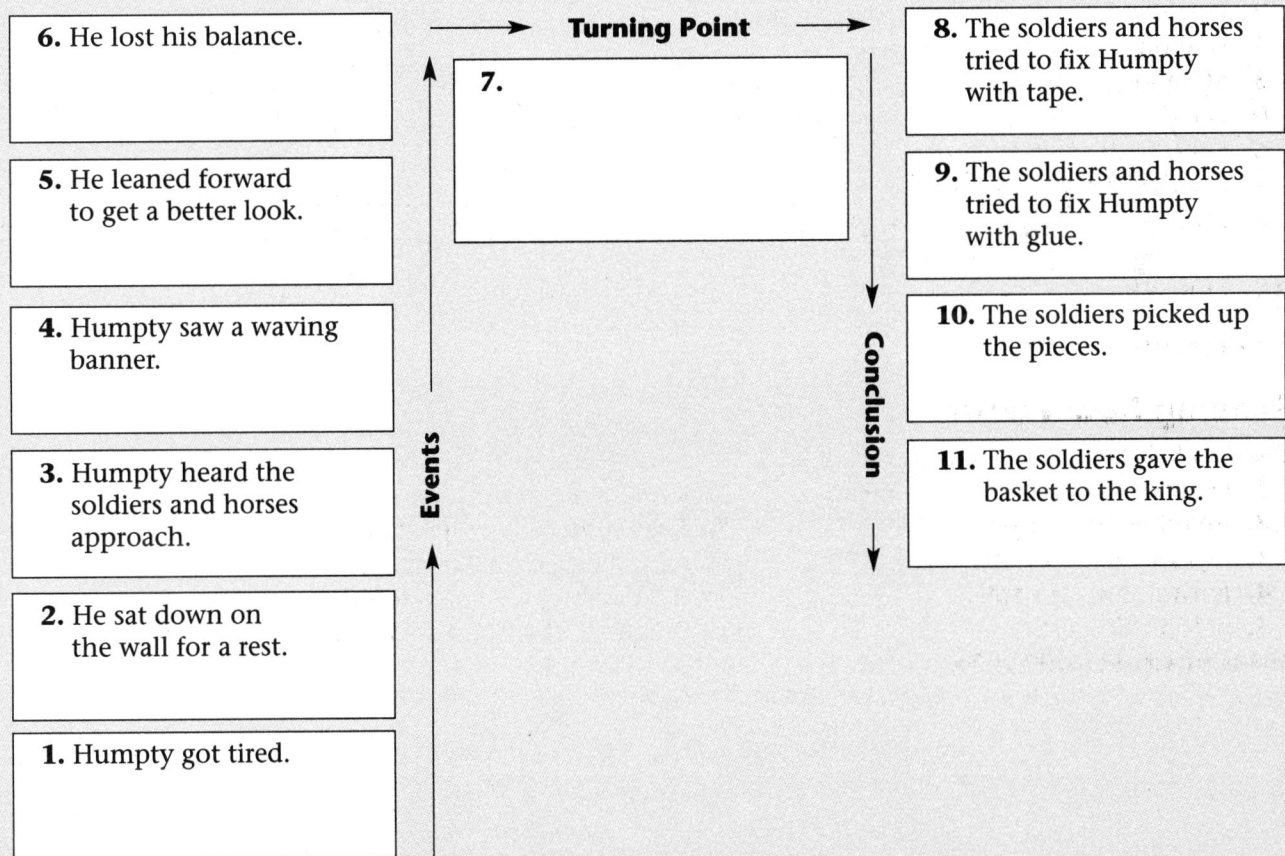

6. He lost his balance.

5. He leaned forward to get a better look.

4. Humpty saw a waving banner.

3. Humpty heard the soldiers and horses approach.

2. He sat down on the wall for a rest.

1. Humpty got tired.

Events

Turning Point

7.

Conclusion

8. The soldiers and horses tried to fix Humpty with tape.

9. The soldiers and horses tried to fix Humpty with glue.

10. The soldiers picked up the pieces.

11. The soldiers gave the basket to the king.

Total possible marks: 10

Mapping a Story

PAGE 38–39 (1 mark for each item. Choose any 5 events from those listed to illustrate.)

1. Title: Chicken Licken
2. Sign "Sherwood Forest"
3. Ducky Lucky at clump of pine trees
4. Road along river
5. Gander Dander on Bridge
6. Sign "London Bridge"
7. Road to meadow
8. Sign "Muffet Meadow"
9. Chicken, Ducky, and Gander sitting by apple tree
10. Chicken, Ducky, and Gander on road to mill
11. Foxy Loxy at the Mill
12. Sign "Floss Mill" on mill
13. Road to wood
14. Sign "Willows Wood"
15. Narrow path in woods
16. Thick clump of bushes in woods.

Total possible marks: 5

Finding Proof of Characteristics

PAGE 40 (1 mark for each answer.)

Characteristic	Proof
1. Nanabush was <u>clever</u>.	a) He set a trap for Eagle.
	b) He gave Eagle the eyes of the dead fish.
2. Eagle was <u>trusting</u>.	He agreed to make a deal with Nanabush.
3. Manitou was <u>kind</u>.	a) He used lightning to give Eagle eyesight.
	b) He burned the net that trapped Eagle.

Total possible marks: 5

Sequencing Events

PAGE 41 (1 mark for each answer.)

3	The North Wind gave the lad a magic cloth that could serve dinner.
4	The landlady stole the cloth and replaced it with an ordinary cloth.
6	The lad went to see the North Wind a second time.
11	The North Wind gave him a stick that could beat when it was told to.
	The lad took the cloth home to his mother but it wouldn't serve dinner.
	The lad told the stick to lay on and it beat the landlord.
14	The landlord gave the magic cloth and the goat back to the lad.
15	The lad told the stick to stop.
16	The lad went home with the North Wind's three gifts.
	The lad went to see the North Wind.
9	The lad took the goat home to his mother but it wouldn't make coins.
	The North Wind gave the lad a goat that could make golden coins.
	The lad went to see the North Wind a third time.
12	The landlord tried to steal the stick.
8	The landlord stole the goat and replaced it with an ordinary goat.

Total possible marks: 10

Checking Word Choice

PAGE 42 (1 mark for each answer.)

1. n<u>ee</u>ded
2. st<u>a</u>ted
3. s<u>e</u>wed
4. <u>de</u>corated
5. a<u>du</u>lts
6. sh<u>i</u>ny
7. r<u>i</u>ng
8. f<u>ie</u>ld
9. thr<u>e</u>w
10. ex<u>ac</u>tly

Total possible marks: 10

Recognizing What Is the Same and What Is Different

PAGE 43 (1 mark for each answer.)

My Comparison Chart of 2 Rhymes		
Title	**Bend a Wire**	**Pat-a-Cake**
Worker	coppersmith	baker
Material Used		
Actions of the Worker	1. swerving 2. curving	patting
What Worker Made	bracelet	cake
What Worker Added		
Who the Worker Made It For	Mama	1. Baby 2. Me

Total possible marks: 10

Analyzing a Story

PAGE 44 (1 mark for each answer. Your answers may be worded a little differently.)

SETTING
By a pond.

TITLE
"The Other Frog Prince"

AUTHOR
Jon Scieszka

CHARACTERS
1. Frog 2. Princess

PROBLEM
Frog needs help to change into a prince.

SOLUTION
Frog asks Princess for help.

EVENTS
1. Frog hops over.
2. Asks princess for a kiss.
3. Princess kisses him.
4. Frog jumps back into pond.
5. Princess wipes her mouth.

Total possible marks: 10

Using Antonyms Meaningfully

PAGE 45 (1 mark for each answer.)

<u>ends</u> **1.** Every good film **begins** with a good story idea.	yes
<u>short</u> **2.** We would decide how **long** Red Riding Hood's hair will be.	yes
<u>dismiss **OR** fire</u> **3.** I then help **hire** the actors who give the characters their voices.	no
<u>silently</u> **4.** The actors read the script **aloud** together.	no
5. The artists would draw where Red Riding Hood and the wolf are to be <u>last</u> placed when they meet in the woods for the **first** time.	yes
<u>few</u> **6.** The animators create **many** drawings of each character's actions.	no
<u>blurry **OR** unclear</u> **7.** The sets of drawings are checked to make sure the movement is **clear**.	no
<u>Before</u> **8.** **After** the drawings are painted, they are filmed onto video tape.	no
<u>under</u> **9.** It takes **over** six months to make Red Riding Hood into a half-hour cartoon	no
<u>easy</u> **10.** It sounds like a lot of **hard** work, and it is.	no

Total possible marks: 20

How Did I Do?

Date	Page(s)	Score	Rating	Why?
	28	/20		
	29	/5		
	30	/20		
	31	/10		
	32–33	/10		
	34	/20		
	35	/5		
	36–37	/10		
	38–39	/5		
	40	/5		
	41	/10		
	42	/10		
	43	/10		
	44	/10		
	45	/20		

Rating: 1 is "easy"; **2** is "somewhat easy"; **3** is "somewhat difficult"; **4** is "difficult"

Beneath the Surface

Classifying Information

PAGE 46 (1 mark for each answer.)

Classifying Creatures				
Animal	**Appearance**	**Home**	**Food**	**Habits**
– triplefin	– orange – glowing stripes	– coral reef	– tiny sea creatures	– uses reef as a "lookout tower"
– octopus	– pinkish-red – sucker-covered arms	– coral reef	– crabs	– uses arms to grab prey
– butterfly fish	– yellow and black – long pointy snout – tiny mouth	– coral reef	– coral polyps	– plucks polyps with nose

Total possible marks: 15

Reading Author Clues

PAGE 47 (1 mark for each answer. Some of your answers may be worded a little differently.)
1. Earthworms have no eyes, no ears, no nose, no teeth, no legs, and no bones.
2. Earthworms avoid light.
3. Worms sense your footsteps.
4. They help it hold tight to its underground burrow if a bird tries to pull the worm out.
5. The pan is smooth and hard to grip with bristles.
6. All kinds of ants are social, which means they live and work together.
7. The worker ants look after the queen and find food.
8. Ants don't usually leave their nests if it's colder than 12°C.
9. Ants can drown in water.
10. An ant can lift 50 times its own weight.

Total possible marks: 10

Organizing Information

PAGES 48–49 (1 mark for each answer.)

Topic: Groundhog	
Title and how it fits: "Afraid of Its Shadow" – so frightened by seeing shadow it goes back to sleep for 6 more weeks	**When it hibernates:** – mid-fall – for about 5–6 months
Where it hibernates: – in underground burrows in flat empty fields	**What happens during hibernation:** – body temperature rises at times – wakes up every 7–10 days – may eat from food store – comes out on Feb. 2 to check shadow

Total possible marks: 10

Reading for Meaning

PAGE 50 (1 mark for each answer.)

1. smiled
2. observe
3. burrowed
4. clever
5. bent

Total possible marks: 5

Interpreting Poem Ideas

PAGE 51 (1 mark for each answer.)

Part A

The shoot pokes through the rich brown soil.	Through earth as rich as brown nut-bread
The oak shoot pushes, stretches, and pokes upwards.	A split, a crack, a baby oak Begins to push and stretch and poke
The shoot grows up past ant and beetle nests.	Past ants at work, Past beetle nooks,
It grows leaves. A tree is born!	Tree coming up—look out ahead!
A green shoot breaks through an acorn seed.	A shoot, a shoot, A greenish boot Kicks open the door Of the acorn house.

Part B

1. The oak shoot pushes, stretches, and pokes upward.
2. As it grows, the shoot passes a worm in its underground home.
3. The shoot grows up past ant and beetle nests.
4. The shoot pokes through the rich brown soil.
5. It grows leaves. A tree is born!

Total possible marks: 10

Checking Details

PAGE 52 (1 mark for each answer.)

1. ~~depths~~ – surface
2. yes
3. ~~unusual~~ – common
4. ~~stalagmites~~ – stalactites
5. yes

Total possible marks: 5

Reading to Remember

PAGE 53 (1 mark for each answer.)
1. Now for as long as anyone can remember everything has been calm and <u>peaceful</u> on the island.
2. Brok hated everything on the island, but most of all he hated the <u>volcano.</u>
3. After many years of wearing away at the rocks, the <u>water</u> finally reached the fiery centre of the volcano.
4. The whole island was <u>smashed</u> to pieces, and even Brok was sent flying through the air.
5. At last, when everything had calmed down, the <u>animals</u> saw that the island had changed completely.
6. <u>Below</u> the waterfall, there was now a beautiful lake, where the pelicans could fish in peace.
7. The volcano too was quiet, and the turtles admired its reflection in the lake as they <u>crawled</u> slowly amongst the stones.
8. Brok the troublemaker had been <u>thrown</u> by the volcano onto the top of a tall tree.
9. A bird took the crab from the tree, thinking he'd make a good <u>supper</u>.
10. I'd like to go to that island one day and see the beautiful lake with its pelicans, and the mountain that was once a <u>volcano</u>.

Total possible marks: 10

Finding Information

PAGE 54 (1 mark for each answer.)
1.	Y	6.	Y
2.	Y	7.	Y
3.	Y	8.	N
4.	Y	9.	Y
5.	N	10.	Y

Total possible marks: 10

Putting Ideas in the Correct Order

PAGE 55 (1 mark for each answer.)

3	All kinds of people came out of the wall, ran around the apartment, and went out the front door.
11	Jonathan told his mother, "There will be no more subways here."
8	Jonathan went to the jam store and carried four cases of blackberry jam back to the old man at City Hall.
2	Jonathan heard a sound coming from behind the wall.
4	Jonathan's mother heard a sound coming from behind the wall.
5	Jonathan went to City Hall and saw the Mayor.
7	Jonathan squeezed in back of the machine and saw a little old man at a very messy desk.
9	Jonathan told the old man where to put the subway station.
10	Jonathan's mother was still standing on the rug because she was stuck to the gum.
6	On his way out of City Hall, Jonathan heard a sound.

Total possible marks: 10

Identifying True Facts

PAGE 56 (1 mark for each answer.)

1. False (page 58)
2. True (page 58)
3. False (page 59)
4. True (page 59)
5. True (page 58)
6. False (page 56)
7. True (page 58)
8. False (page 59)
9. False (page 59)
10. False (page 59)

Total possible marks: 10

Matching Words and Meanings

PAGE 57 (1 mark for each answer.)

1. herbivores
2. scientist
3. warm-blooded
4. carnivores
5. exhibition
6. cold-blooded
7. fossil
8. Mesozoic
9. prehistoric
10. quarry

Total possible marks: 10

Organizing Information in a Chart

PAGES 58–99 (1 mark for each answer.)

	People	Places	Things
1. the greatest gold rush in history			✓
2. adventurers from all over the world	✓		
3. where the Yukon and Klondike Rivers come together		✓	
4. more than a billion dollars			✓
5. the frozen north		✓	
6. steamships			✓
7. rubber boots, cotton goods, and hot water bottles			✓
8. the Yukon		✓	
9. Belinda Mulroney	✓		
10. the Klondike		✓	

Total possible marks: 10

Comparing Ideas

PAGES 60–61 (1 mark for each answer.)

	"Far-away Mysteries"	"Our Solar System"
1. tells about the planets	✓	✓
2. makes you wonder about the planets	✓	✓
3. gives facts	✓	✓
4. asks a question	✓	
5. is like a story	✓	
6. tells you that the Sun doesn't move	✓	✓
7. is fact		✓
8. is imaginative	✓	
9. tells you that the planets move around the Sun	✓	✓
10. names an astronomer's instrument	✓	

Total possible marks: 15

How Did I Do?

Date	Page(s)	Score	Rating	Why?
	46	/15		
	47	/10		
	48–49	/10		
	50	/5		
	51	/10		
	52	/5		
	53	/10		
	54	/10		
	55	/10		
	56	/10		
	57	/10		
	58–59	/10		
	60–61	/15		

Rating: 1 is "easy"; **2** is "somewhat easy"; **3** is "somewhat difficult"; **4** is "difficult"

Super Senses!

Writing Questions

PAGE 62 (1 mark for each answer. Some of your answers may be worded a little differently.)
1. What does the morning mist look like?
2. What do I wiggle?
3. Where does Grandfather stop the canoe?
4. What does Grandfather stretch out?
5. Where are the four loons?
6. What decorates the male loon's back?
7. What does the mother loon have on her back?
8. What is my heart doing?
9. How does the loon dive?
10. What is the morning on the lake?

Total possible marks: 10

Finding Proof of the Author's Feelings

PAGE 63 (1 mark for any **5** of the following answers.)
   – bright yellow colour
   – wonderful picture
   – just like the sun
   – beautiful bouquet
   – bright yellow
   – nothing can make you feel as happy
   – dancing in the breeze

Total possible marks: 5

Matching Words with Photographs

PAGE 64 (1 mark for each answer.)
1. bright colours
2. every face is unique
3. repeating patterns of reflections
4. a collection
5. your pet's unique character

Total possible marks: 5

Organizing Information

PAGE 65 (1 mark for each answer.)

Characters	Setting	Puzzle (Crime)
• Tracy • Angie • David • Prince	• detective agency • Tracy's garage • first day of summer vacation	• missing skateboard
Suspects • David • Prince	**Motive (Reason)** • jealousy • winning a skateboard contest	**Clues** • long brown scratch • grass • dog hairs

Total possible marks: 15

Knowing What Happens Next

PAGE 66 (1 mark for each answer.)

2. g		**7.** a	
3. f		**8.** k	
4. c		**9.** b	
5. h		**10.** j	
6. i		**11.** e	

Total possible marks: 10

Deciding Who, What, Why, When, Where, or How

PAGE 67 (1 mark for each answer.)

1. what		**6.** when	
2. why		**7.** who	
3. how		**8.** where	
4. where		**9.** how	
5. why		**10.** what	

Total possible marks: 10

Understanding a Story Pattern

PAGES 68–69 (1 mark for each item you should show in your picture or write down.)

In your first picture, you should show:
- a blue sky
- birds in trees
- flowers in gardens
- children playing in the playground

In your second picture, you should show:
- the children looking up
- flowers with closed petals
- birds sitting on the tree brances with their faces under their wings
- wind
- grey clouds
- the sun hiding behind the clouds

Total possible marks: 10

Choosing the Best Sentence Endings

PAGE 70 (1 mark for each answer.)
1. a) had a face as round as the moon
2. c) she made them think of the blossoms that covered the lake
3. c) could not hear or learn to speak
4. c) blossom
5. c) walk with the graceful birds
6. b) the queen and king
7. a) "She will learn to dance."
8. c) patiently
9. b) the pleasure and delight in the eyes of the people
10. c) the most famous dancer in the Khmer kingdom

Total possible marks: 10

Using Illustrations

PAGE 71 (1 mark for each answer.)
1. c) Dava couldn't herd the sheep very well.
2. b) The sheep thought Dava was a tree so they chewed on his sash.
3. c) Dava played the flute.
4. a) Still whistling, Dava led the sheep toward the sheepcote.
   e) The sheep were calm and Dava was calm.

Total possible marks: 5

Finding Specific Information

PAGE 72 (1 mark for each answer.)

1. sound	6. bones
2. vibrations	7. brain
3. vibrating	8. dogs
4. molecules	9. air
5. invisible	10. movement

Total possible marks: 10

Checking Information

PAGE 73 (1 mark for each answer.)

1. ~~Canada~~ – Africa	6. ~~her~~ – his
2. ~~after~~ – before	7. ~~half~~ – whole
3. ~~month~~ – week	8. ~~never~~ – always
4. ~~circles~~ – stripes	9. ~~cool~~ – hot
5. ~~mother~~ – grandmother	10. ~~hamburgers~~ – hotdogs

Total possible marks: 10

Following a Recipe

PAGES 74–75 (1 mark for each answer.)

1. ingredients	5. three
2. directions	6. Mozzarella
3. onions, pepperoni, and sliced mushrooms (1 mark for each.)	7. mini
	8. sliced
4. enjoy!	

Total possible marks: 10

Classifying Details

PAGES 76–77 (1 mark for each answer.)

__D__ put a strainer over the mouth of the jar
__N__ hot tap water
__L__ fog will start to form on the inside of the jar
__N__ a strainer
__D__ pour out all the water except for 25 mm
__N__ several ice cubes
__D__ fill the strainer with ice cubes
__N__ a large jar or a wide-mouthed bottle
__D__ watch for a while
__D__ fill the jar with hot water

Total possible marks: 10

Understanding Similes

PAGES 78–79 (1 mark for each pair in the "What's Being Compared" columns. 1 mark for each answer in the last column. Your answers may be worded a little differently.)

What's Being Compared		What They Have in Common
1. hands	ice	cold
2. jumbo jet	eagle	soared
3. jacket	shoe	comfortable
4. Canadian Prairies	pancake	flat
5. candy	rock	hard
6. Rashif	bear	hungry
7. Marissa	bump on a log	sat
8. teacher	owl	wise
9. hail	golf balls	loud
10. cake	pieces of broken stone	crumbled

Total possible marks: 20

Finding Information

PAGE 80 (1 mark for each answer.)

1. whip-poor-will
2. blue goatfish
3. walruses and seals (2 marks)
4. blue goatfish
5. lion's mane jellyfish
6. blue catfish
7. walruses and seals (2 marks)
8. humans
9. owlet nightjar
10. owlet nightjar
11. owlet nightjar
12. lion's mane jellyfish
13. blue catfish

Total possible marks: 15

How Did I Do?

Date	Page(s)	Score	Rating	Why?
	62	/10		
	63	/5		
	64	/5		
	65	/15		
	66	/10		
	67	/10		
	68–69	/10		
	70	/10		
	71	/5		
	72	/10		
	73	/10		
	74–75	/10		
	76–77	/10		
	78–79	/20		
	80	/15		

Rating: 1 is "easy"; **2** is "somewhat easy"; **3** is "somewhat difficult"; **4** is "difficult"

Carving New Frontiers

Identifying Characters, Setting, and Storyline

PAGE 81 (1 mark for each answer.)

1. c) Pettranella
2. c) long ago in Manitoba
3. a) how a family settled in a new country
4. b) sad and excited
5. c) a big boat
6. c) geese flying north
7. b) ox cart
8. b) spring came
9. b) a small cabin
10. c) happily, because Pettranella was able to keep her promise to her grandmother

Total possible marks: 10

Using a Timeline

PAGES 82–83 (1 mark for each answer.)

1. c) refrigerator
2. c) vacuum cleaner
3. a) television
4. b) DVDs
5. 1876
6. Velcro
7. vacuum cleaner
8. refrigerator
9. sliced bread
10. electric guitar – 1921

Total possible marks: 10

Finding Information in Illustrations

PAGE 84 (1 mark for each answer.)

1. a) shovel
   b) hats
2. a) salt
   b) barrels
3. a) barrels
   b) nothing
4. a) a lantern
   b) 10
5. a) 5
   b) his mother (Mama)
6. a) a book
   b) happy
7. a) a candle
   b) the alphabet
8. a) his left foot
   b) on the ground
   c) very happy
9. a) the boy's name
   b) right-handed
   c) on the ground

Total possible marks: 20

Finding Words That Go Together

PAGE 85 (1 mark for each answer.)

1. bunches
2. inside
3. today
4. everything
5. myself
6. white
7. store
8. bunches
9. kegs
10. jars
11. balls
12. packets
13. tins
14. bolts
15. bunches

Total possible marks: 15

Making Good Guesses

PAGE 86 (1 mark for every correctly drawn line.)

Column A   **Column B**

Two-Feather was lonely because   the sun.

Two-Feather slept a lot because   he wanted to forget how lonely he was.

Two-Feather had never seen fire because   there was no one around.

Instead of fire, Two-Feather used   his hands.

To dig out the roots from under the   no one knew how to make it.
snow, Two-Feather used

4. (1 mark for each answer.)
   a) the water in the stream
   b) soft moss
   c) his feet
   d) two sticks
   e) the forest

Total possible marks: 10

Finding Specific Information

PAGE 87 (1 mark for each answer. Your answers may be worded a little differently.)
1. Many important discoveries were first made <u>in China.</u>
2. Paper was first made <u>more than two thousand years ago.</u>
3. The paper sheets were hung up <u>to finish drying.</u>
4. A lodestone <u>would always turn until it pointed north and south.</u>
5. Fishers used <u>kites to carry their fishing lines.</u>
6. The Chinese used lodestone to <u>tell them direction.</u>
7. The author is <u>Sharon Stewart.</u>
8. The Chinese invented porcelain <u>a long time ago.</u>
9. The cocoons of silkworms were soaked <u>in hot water.</u>
10. When the Chinese made paper, <u>the pulp was left behind on the screen.</u>

Total possible marks: 10

Recognizing Text Formats

PAGES 88–89 (1 mark for each answer. Your answers may be worded a little differently.)
1. d) questions and answers
2. b) they're printed in **bold**
   c) they end with a question mark
   d) they are usually shorter than the answers
3. b) A
4. d) where
5. The Wright Brothers, **OR** Orville and Wilbur Wright
6. When there is enough air pressure on the bottom of the wing.
7. An ornithopter.
8. Because of air pressure.

Total possible marks: 10

Checking Details

PAGE 90 (1 mark for each answer.)

1. ~~years~~ – a while
2. ~~city~~ – town
3. ~~days~~ – months
4. ~~afternoon~~ – noon
5. ~~brick~~ – clay
6. ~~house~~ – job
7. ~~mystery~~ – adventure
8. ~~earlier~~ – later
9. ~~disagreed~~ – agreed
10. ~~think~~ – imagine

Total possible marks: 10

Knowing Fact from Fiction

PAGE 91 (1 mark for each answer.)

1. fiction
2. fiction
3. fact
4. fiction
5. fact

Total possible marks: 5

Finding Missing Information

PAGE 92 (1 mark for each answer.)

1. Sam's diary begins on <u>May</u> 24 and ends on June <u>15</u>.
2. On May 24, Sam wrote about his last day at <u>school</u> with his <u>friends</u>.
3. May 25: Sam wrote about how sick everyone was feeling, except for his <u>mom</u>.
4. On May 27, all Sam was able to write was "<u>Sick</u> today!"
5. May 29: Sam writes that all the sails have been <u>reefed</u>.
6. On June 6, Sam wrote that Charlie had found a <u>friend</u>, Sam couldn't see for almost a <u>week</u>, and that Charlie and Sam had been reading about <u>albatrosses</u>.
7. June 7: Sam thinks they get to Hawaii in about a <u>week</u>.
8. On June 12, Sam writes that it was too cold a week before and that it's almost too <u>hot</u> now!
9. On June 14, Sam is so excited. He writes: "I CAN'T <u>WAIT</u>!!!"
10. June 15, Sam wrote that after exactly <u>three</u> weeks at sea, he's not sure if he'll even be able to <u>walk</u> properly on land again.

Total possible marks: 15

Matching Words and Meanings

PAGE 93 (1 mark for each answer.)

1. shuffled
2. homeland
3. perch
4. fluttered
5. hammock

Total possible marks: 5

Identifying Authors and Illustrators

PAGE 94 (1 mark for each answer.)

1. d) Sonali
2. c) Rachel
3. c) Akanksha
4. b) Meadhbh
5. a) Peta
   b) Cheryl
   c) Constanza
   d) Mayra
   e) Kathryn
6. a) Vicky – Greece
   b) Renato – Peru
   c) Samantha – Australia
7. a) Samantha – 11
   b) Fortunate – 7
   c) Peta – 12

Total possible marks: 15

How Did I Do?

Date	Page(s)	Score	Rating	Why?
	81	/10		
	82–83	/10		
	84	/20		
	85	/15		
	86	/10		
	87	/10		
	88–89	/10		
	90	/10		
	91	/5		
	92	/15		
	93	/5		
	94	/15		

Rating: 1 is "easy"; **2** is "somewhat easy"; **3** is "somewhat difficult"; **4** is "difficult"